THE MONSTER WITHIN

Mary Ellen Aschenbrenner

A Handlebar Publications

ISBN: 978-0-9976575-2-4

A HANDLEBAR PUBLICATIONS
P.O. Box 313
Somonauk, IL 60552

More to Come

TERRORS AND TRAVELS

She's a columnist for the Joliet Spectator. Editor Molly Zelko disappears—likely at the hands of the Mafia. "You can't scare me."

As a Joliet Herald News Correspondent, she's told, "Remember what happened to Molly."

Mary Ellen travels the world, meets officials, statesmen, the gifted, and the deranged. She encounters ghosts and thwarts an abduction. Tangling with police chiefs, embezzlers, spirits, and the KBG (Bulgaria's secret police), fall into her job description. Being told, "You'll be murdered and raped—in that order," pummels her limits and raises the hair on her head.

BORN TO BE A STAR

(Still) Floating in a Galaxy of Hot Air
Volume Two

Mary Ellen continues the humor of
Born to be Star Volume One

What Others Say

The … Monster … Within

Monsters hide in dark places. Mary Ellen Aschenbrenner's book flings open all doors and windows. It flushes Monster from the shadows. *The Monster Within* is real—about real people addressing pain and anguish. It meets commonly-held, entrenched stigmas head-on.

"*The Monster Within* doesn't shy from the uncomfortable. Monsters burrow in hearts, souls, minds, and bodies. Light must flood them so those who experience them can have joy beyond sorrow, hope beyond fear, and life beyond death."
Pastor David Fosco, East-West Church, Aurora, IL

***

"*The Monster Within* unlocks the gashes of mental illness and erases stigmas so others may understand and families may heal. The man in the story was not the Uncle Mike we all knew. The man we knew was robust with a grandiose smile and a contagious laugh. He so loved. And, I so loved that man filled with unconditional devotion and affection."
Alice Bertagnoli Reigh

***

"From a professional view - *The Monster Within* is a real-life horror story—a confession of pain, torment, love, and persistence in the face of what seemed like a never-ending tragedy. Wonderfully written and enlightening. (continued)

"Personally - Having lived the pages of *The Monster Within*, I know how bad life became. It makes me exceedingly grateful for my family and friends. The book is wonderfully, even masterfully, written, Mom ... but since I experienced it, it was one of the hardest reads of my life. Well done. It will be tough to beat this one." **Michael E. Aschenbrenner**

This book is nonfiction. Characters are real. When possible, actual names are used. In some instances, names are omitted or first names only appear. Information shared in the book is not meant to substitute for professional, personal medical care for any individual(s). Information contained in this work is strictly the author's opinions based on the author's current research.

A Handlebar Publications
P.O. Box 313
Somonauk, IL 60552
Handlebar07@gmail.com
First Edition: July 2019

The author and publisher are not responsible for websites or their contents not owned by the publisher, Library of Congress Cataloging-in-Publication Data, Aschenbrenner, Mary Ellen.
ISBN: 978-0-9976575-2-4

Mike in early days. Appliance salesman for Northern Illinois Gas Company. Downtown Joliet, IL

The Monster Within

By
Mary Ellen Aschenbrenner

With a Foreword
by
Michael J. Stephen, Ph.D.

Cancer strikes one in every two men and one in every three women. Additionally, every year, one-in-five adults worldwide experience addiction, a mental illness, or personality disorder ... depression, narcissism, schizophrenia, bipolar disease—even a brain tumor. The list is endless. No family escapes the horrors.

According to the National Brain Tumor Society, in the United States alone, more than 190,000 people are diagnosed with a brain tumor each year. The median age at diagnosis is 58.

For all of you, your families, and your caregivers: "May you see God's light through this darkness. The journey will be long and devastating no matter how brief. You are not alone. I share your tears."

It was like an octopus squeezing his brain.

Editor

Allison Rott

Leave life better than you find it!
MaryEllen Aschenbrenner

The Monster Within

Mary Ellen Aschenbrenner

About the Author

Mary Ellen Aschenbrenner, author, speaker, columnist, and award-winning feature writer has been published throughout the Midwest and in New York. Known as Joliet's Erma Bombeck, she departs from her humor forte' in *The Monster Within* to share the gut-wrenching story of her family's encounter with brain cancer.

Published first at 14, she has written and co-written hundreds of articles for newspapers and periodicals. Four books are to her credit since 2009. She tells all ... personal and professional. In novels to come, she divulges coercions and threats. She exposes criminal intent. She's told, if she doesn't shut her mouth, she'll be murdered and raped—in that order.

She motivates audiences to face life straight on, smile amid adversities, and trust in a Higher Power. Her mission is to put joyful beams on depressed faces, foster hope in those who have lost courage, and not to die with stories still in her. A member of In Print Professional Writers, The

Chicago Writers Guild, Word Weavers, and the Erma Bombeck Workshop, Aschenbrenner shares with writers, civic, philanthropic, and support groups. She facilitates a writers' group in Somonauk, IL.

Publications: *Born to be a Star Floating in A Galaxy of Hot Air,* available through A Handlebar Publications and Amazon; *Dellwood Chronicles* by Dr. Reno Caneva (with Aschenbrenner), available at www.dellwoodchronicles.com; *Celebrate 100/50/50*, private distribution.

Books to Come: *Terrors and Travels* and *Born to be a Star, Vol. 2 (Still Floating in Hot Air)*

This can't be real … but it is

Life is a Testimony

Table of Contents

Acknowledgments

Editor Allison Rott ... With gifts abundant, you gave words when ports emptied. You strengthened when I weakened and invaded my soul ... you picked up my pen and wrote lyrics. I adore you ... and your red pen. The Somonauk Library Writers Group and Word Weavers—your input pulled me through. Graphic artist Larissa Barbee, your skills are evident. You are a pleasure and a joy. Lynn and Bill Locasto ... when they heard of Mike's illness, they came to the lake and shot family photos (shown in this book). They refused payment. Your gift is a gift of love and memories.

Thanks, praise, and acknowledgments are insufficient though sincere ... Mike's sister Rosella, Mike's brothers Joe and Bob, and their spouses, Bud, Hazel, and Marge ... and "like brother and sister to all Aschenbrenners," Dale and Norma Olson ...

I pray this revelation will not tear holes in anyone's heart. Mike did not bring this sorrow. It was the Monster within. The book exposes the Monster of mental and brain disfunctions so readers understand what others endure.

My sister Freda provided nourishment while her husband Ed made our bath handicapped accessible. He refused payment. My sister Lois and friend Colleen Caviness offered to rescue my Mom from experiencing this malady.

More acts of unending kindness—Denny Stevens, Barb and Don Slaby, Georgine and Steve Platko, and Jeanne and Ed Albrecht!

NICOR friends, the Carpentiers, Gene and Pat, and so many others who stepped up for union meetings and treatments. Mike Rogan, whose blessed voice brought joy to our wedding and cleansing tears to Mike's celebration of life. Mike Steven, wrote Mike's eulogy and penned this book's Foreword. Words tenderly written and spoken. Friends and neighbors, Dale and Kay Smith ... your generosity gave respite to hurting bodies. Childhood playmate Paul Mussario and wife Judy ... your lifelong friendship and weekly cards encouraged and consoled as did cards from many others.

Dr. Martin Brauweiler guided and protected. Dr. George Hadley spoke truth—total honesty. He said what he would do if faced with a deadly brain tumor.

Wonderful Hospice workers who compassionately cared for Mike. Terry, the bereavement counselor, who rescued me from Post-Traumatic Stress-Disorder. You are angels in scrubs. Within hours of Mike's death, you (Hospice) delivered a beautiful red rose to my door. It sat preserved at my bedside for months. Financial advisor Mike Lukas, you became Mike's friend and remained mine.

Many not acknowledged—I thank all for being faithful and fulfilling needs. Irreplaceable—all who took part in Mike's short life. You, too, are in this book.

And the last are truly first! Steadfast mother Marian, my children Michael, Amy, and Janet, sons-in-law Mark and John, and former daughter-in-law Alice. Without your sacrifice and your charitable hearts, I could not have endured.

While Michael in Hebrew means "Gift from God," I acknowledge all three of my children are "Gifts from God." May He abundantly reward all of you.

It is finished.

Fondly … and tearfully …

Mary Ellen

Foreword

by

Michael J. Steven, Ph.D.

Cancer is serious business. Brain cancer is especially insidious and ravaging. "The Monster," as Mary Ellen Aschenbrenner aptly labels it, entered her family's lives and wreaked havoc. It shattered relationships for a time—traumatized their entire family.

How these two good people handled its onset, progression, and the final ending is the guts of this story. Everyone, especially those facing tragedy or serious illness, will benefit from this book. I encourage you to read it. When Mary Ellen asked me to read her manuscript and write this Foreword, she cautioned, "As my Mike's dear friend, you likely won't enjoy it. I lay it all out."

Lay it out ... she did, with clarity and unsparing honesty. Her husband, Mike, and I were the best of friends since high school. We played tennis together, went to parties together, drank beer, ate pizza—and got in trouble together. So, I can't say one enjoys reading about two good friends' difficult and heart-wrenching struggle to cope with devastating brain cancer. However, I am moved, instructed, and inspired. You will be as well.

The Monster Within

Prelude

A few strokes of an artist's brush and life would have been a Renoir'. The future had been impeccably calculated and strategically scheduled.

In the shadows, a creature called Monster splattered an unsettling sketch on his palate, a scheme to shatter those plans. Powers beyond comprehension. Death his intent.

Monster waited. He seeped through cracks leaving us emotionally handcuffed and shackled. The exact date he slipped in was not documented. However, Mike's outlandish actions leave one to believe, Mike's senses were seized long before I became suspect. Monster's thunderous tones were horrors of doom and appeared and disappeared intermittently. He was real and he lived within.

Some days, Mike would mow the lawn twice, making sure the cuts were exact and evenly spaced. God forbid a weed grow in his garden, his car have a spot, his bed not be made to perfection, or whiskers bloom on his chin. Sometimes, he'd vanish for hours; claim he'd been shopping. Yet, had nothing to show for his excursions.

Other days, things did not matter. He was the rational man I had married. Existence became yin and yang, Jekyll and

Hyde. The moments between Jekyll and Hyde were wonderful. Mike laughed at the wind, loved me unquestionably, and gave the fruits of his garden to neighbors and co-workers. Neighborhood children called him the Vegetable Bunny. His grandchildren called him Popee.

The times of sanity were ports of peace—brief stays easing the slashes of hateful charades. Pleasurable moments were often seconds; some minutes. On occasion, they lingered lovingly for days. They were flashes of harmony that sadly dissipated like dew on morning grass.

You ask how I did not realize Monster had entered our bed. Mike and I existed in cocoons; neither of us sharing concerns and the evil creature never stayed long enough for us to discover his name. But, we knew something ...

A good marriage is worth fighting for and fight we did. Mike had become obsessive, compulsive, and paranoid schizophrenic—mentally sick and deranged.

I was mean. I wore bitterness well. Yet, I labored to capture glimpses of Mike's former wit and now hidden wisdom, often covering up in public by painting a rosy tint on his embittered tongue.

I clung relentlessly to the towel until it became too heavy to throw and then said, "No more."

I Beyond Comprehension

CHAPTER 1

The Fox and Pillars of Concrete

He slammed the pedal to the floor. My heart, tumbling like an acrobat lodged crosswise in my throat. The barren trees on the left became pillars of concrete while the angry Fox River on my right took voice, "Join me."

From one side of the road to the other the car wheeled. Rocks, broken limbs, and rotted debris hurled through the air.

"My God! What are you doing? That's the wrong way. You're heading east. Go west! For God's sake! Slow down ..."

"If you're so damned smart, you get us home." My once loving spouse screeched. Brutally strong, his face reddened. His eyes swelled beyond their hollows ... his shout spawned a biting sting. I clasped my hands over my ears. His shrill originated in Satan's Den. It pierced my soul.

"God! You're trying to kill us."

I screamed repeatedly while seizing the wheel from his gritted fists. "You're possessed."

Forest on one side. A gushing stream on the other. Death sang her song as Mike, dazed as though drunk, loosened his hold on the steering wheel and let up on the pedal. In seconds, composure returned, and he drove three miles to our Lake Holiday home.

We had had thirty-five years of a good marriage. Year thirty-six varied and year thirty-seven paralleled hell. Where his mood perched or what might set him off was uncertain and rapidly changed. While his pain was his own, he made it mine. What happened to the man I married?

I had arrived home from work that Friday during Lent greeted by a lawn resembling a golf course. Mike had edged the long drive, trimmed bushes, and blown every blade of grass off the blacktop. It likely took all day. I expected to see him sprawled in his recliner with a martini in hand, too exhausted to move, and eager for me or my mom who lived with us to prepare dinner.

A manicured house also awaited. Dishes were done, beds made, floors scrubbed, carpets vacuumed. Lemon Pledge permeated the house. Likewise, Mike exuded fresh—showered, teeth brushed, hair combed. Rested, he smelled of Bay Rum cologne, dressed in spotless, crisp, pressed clothes. Mike's shirts never bore spots down the front like mine.

He spoke in complete sentences. Unusual. As of late, his conversations were less than three words, "yes, no, do this, do that."

"I told your Mom not to bother with dinner. Let's go out for walleye," he perked the minute I walked in. I agreed. A pleasant night seemed to be ahead. I treasured pleasant nights.

He didn't speak on the ride to the restaurant making it a delightful drive. Spring awaited. Burgundy trillium and white bloodroot lit the forest while woodland flowers poked their noses through decayed leaves and puffs of lingering winter snow. The recent time change in Illinois gave an extra hour to enjoy the burgeoning forest. Barren trees were eager to burst with new life. I envied their new life.

Across the road, the Fox River overfilled above cold, hard banks. Her wailing, mad waters sirened for company. The Fox and I had much in common—we were angry.

The small-town restaurant, crowded with Lake Holiday residents and farmers who recognized a dinner bargain, served fresh walleye. Mike ordered a martini.

"If you have another, I will drive home," I said. Mike nodded in agreement as he never resisted my request to drive when he drank.

Mike's eyes suddenly danced from side to side scanning the diners. He leaned across the table. His breath tickled my ear, "Look at 'those' people. The nerve. They're stealing food."

"What are you babbling about? What people?" I asked searching for the meaning.

"Over there—they're just taking the food. They're not paying for it."

"That's the salad bar, macaroni, lettuce, beets. How many martinis did you have before I got home? I think we can add the salad bar to dinner. Why don't you ask the gentleman behind you? He helped himself."

"I can't do that! That would be rude! What's the matter with you?"

I shook my head, rose, and walked to the table behind Mike. "Excuse me, is the salad bar extra or is it included with the meal?"

"Just two bucks extra on Fridays," he responded shoving salad into his mouth.

"You are insolent and brazen! I can't believe you did that." Mike was florid. Appalled. He was articulate and not one bit quiet.

Again, I am like a rose trampled on the ground. It happens often as of late.

He pushed our table aside, strode to the salad bar, and filled his plate to overflowing.

My turn for mortification. The rest of the dinner was peaceful and silent ... if you call silent peaceful.

CHAPTER 2

More Than a Nightmare

An unsettling dream became frequent. Eggs of every size covered our bedroom floor. Edging between them so as not to crack their shells and awaken Mike required the dexterity of a ballerina. Over time, something or someone spread more and more eggs for me to slither through. I'd stumble. Fear overpowered and I'd fall. Eggs shattered. Shells flew everywhere. With eyes hard as granite, a silhouette of Mike then surfaced and shook me with brutal force.

A delusion? Hallucination? A premonition? It terrified me. I'd awaken to a house of disarray littered in ugly.

It was a dream. Life was not. It would take threats of murder and suicide for me to confront the Monster within.

Mom and I discussed Mike's rash behaviors and wondered if he had become an alcoholic, had early-onset dementia, or other mental issues. Mom searched upstairs when Mike wasn't around. I scoured the basement and garage. We found no telltale empty bottles or glasses, no sign of excessive drinking. He consumed only a nightly martini and an occasional beer. After reading how it is possible to have an alcoholic personality without being an alcoholic, my daughter Amy and I attended Al-Anon, a support organization for those whose lives are affected by alcohol. We hoped to glean insight on how we should react to someone with alcoholic traits.

Mike also developed habits of grabbing and squeezing me inappropriately in public or in my mother's presence—all the while, he chastised me for being a prude. Things he never did before. He became hypersexual. I chalked it up to his being rested and retired, expecting it to lessen as retirement went on. It did not.

There were other signs. Signals hindsight admits ... hugging our daughters in a too familiar way. (Does my imagination run overtime?) Mike would never. He was always, always a gentleman. However, our daughters Amy and Janet expressed concern. There were times Mike couldn't discern his daughters from me, his wife.

On one of my sister Freda's visits, she was alone with Mike in the living room while I worked downstairs. I didn't hear the details of their conversation.

After Freda left, Mike came to the kitchen with a boastful smile plastered across his face.

"I got your sister told."

"What do you mean?"

"I got her told how she didn't do her share of taking care of your mother. How she dumps everything on you and it isn't fair!"

"Hold on there! I don't have issues with my sister. She doesn't live with Mom. She's an hour and a half away in Joliet. Your expectations are unjustified. You were the one who insisted on taking Mom in. I have never regretted your decision, but you have no right to interfere with my family. If I have issues with my sisters, I handle them. When your sister cared for your mother and you and your brothers took your mom on weekends, I never once interfered. It was your place to handle your family. It's my place to handle mine. Period."

He seemed sad and said, "I thought I was helping you. You work so hard for your Mom and I thought ..."

"No," I retorted, "You didn't think. You didn't consider how you made my sister feel."

Although Mom was on oxygen and frail, she cooked dinner during the week when I worked. She'd start early each morning, prepare one item and then, rest before returning to make another. On weekends, the kitchen was mine.

I overheard Mom tell a friend, "I can't do much to help around here, but I try to do at least one thing for Mary

Ellen and one thing for Mike every day. It's the least I can do." Utterly amazing for an 84-year-old with heart failure.

One evening after Freda's visit, Mom took me aside and said she wouldn't prepare meals anymore. The last thing I wanted to do after work was to come home and cook. I pleaded with her to continue. She relented and met me halfway. "I'll cook for us, but I won't cook for him."

Further prodding revealed Mike would take his half-eaten plate of food and scrape it into the garbage in front of Mom and then, make a sandwich or grill another steak. Their compatibility deteriorated beyond repair.

In desperation, I called Amy. "I'm at wit's end trying to please your dad. You always seem to get through to him. Can you have a talk with him?"

She came later that day and sat with her dad in the living room. During a commercial break, she asked how retirement was progressing and if he had caught any walleye for Grandma. At one intermission, she said, "You have to quit being mean to Mom and Grandma."

"You don't understand, he said, they're poisoning me. Putting metal in my food."

Sadness and desperation inked his face. In a mute appeal for sympathy through eyes that spoke great sorrow, his chin dropped.

Amy insisted he was wrong and offered to taste his food to prove it wasn't contaminated … shades of dinner with Henry the Eighth.

Weeping softly, he mouthed it again, "You … you just don't understand. They're poisoning me."

Even soft-spoken Amy could not permeate his walls. Mike acts strangely. Yet, normal—most of the time.

Another day, I came into the dining area where I had laid stories on the table in readiness to take to Ottawa. As an Ottawa Times correspondent and feature writer, I contributed to the newspaper on a regular basis. Spread on top of my stories were clothes taken from the washing machine. Water ran from the table onto the floor. An ogre invaded the room. It ruined the stories. Mike seemed not to perceive the damage.

"Why did you do this? What possessed you? Do you have any idea how many hours I spent printing out those stories on that old, stubborn printer?"

A sick grin covered his face. It breathed provocation. His tone, high-pitched and sarcastic, taunted, "Why, I thought I was helping you." His words burnt, moving me to furry and maddened response, but I held back.

"And, what do you think you can do about it?" He grinned.

His glare gave the eye what the ear did not hear. I gulped; perspiration popped on my forehead. He was a curious mixture of brash and bizarre. I wanted to dump the entire mess, table and all, on his head—but that would be insane and I'd have to clean that up, too.

"Are you really that mean or are you totally deranged?" I asked. Then, I answered for him. "Yes, you really are that damn mean."

One more time, he was "helping me."

A week later, Mom called me at work. "You need to come home right away. Mike is on the parkway next door with Lake Holiday board members. His eyes inch. His arms thrust at them like spears. It's getting out of hand. I'm afraid. He has guns!"

I couldn't leave work as Human Resources was short-handed, and I relieved the switchboard for breaks. I loved my job at Henry Pratt Valve Company as the work varied. I was part of Human Resources, but bounced between departments to fill voids. It kept me from thinking about the hazards of home.

"I'm an hour away, Mom. Mike would never ..." I stopped.

Members of the Lake Holiday board and a contractor were busying themselves canvassing the lot next door to determine appropriateness for a gravel and stone storage site for a shoreline preservation project. It would be ongoing for several summers or until they secured the lake's seven miles of shoreline. The green area beside our lot would no longer be viable for picnics and fishing. Instead, it would become a dusty gravel pit.

It would ruin one of the prettiest spots on the lake. This park-like setting next door was a major reason we had chosen our home. Likewise, the contractor found it perfect for storing gravel and machinery as it was midway on the lake with a gentle slope.

Weeks earlier, we had begged the board to reject the location. My mom, with one lung and congestive heart failure, plus the man across the street with emphysema, lung cancer, and dementia would suffer from excessive dust. Both were on oxygen and this likely would be their last summer. The dust from a gravel pit in their midst would force them to remain indoors for the rest of their limited lives.

When Mike saw the board survey the land, his curiosity peaked and diplomacy went out the window. Uninvited, he joined the officials as they inspected the grounds and he took matters into his own hands. Tempers blazed.

"Mary Ellen, things are heated." Mom was frantic. "I've never seen Mike rage like this. Please come home. He's dangerous."

I left work.

Mike was reading the paper when I walked in. "What's going on?" I asked hoping things hadn't been as volatile as Mom had said.

He lowered the paper. "Don't concern yourself. I handled the greenway. The city fathers were here. I took care of things."

Nice, complete, short sentences. Then, with paper covering his brow, he enunciated each word with measured, perfect cadence, "I – am – going - to – castrate – each – and – every – one – of –them – and ... I told them so."

Was he losing his mind? Or was I? A week later, I left Mike at home and attended the lake's board meeting where the contractor announced he would not use the greenway next to our home.

"The neighbor next door is dangerous. I would fear for our workers and their equipment."

Board members grinned.

CHAPTER 3

Changes in Persona

Mike became additionally attentive to his person. For years, we begged him to get hearing aids. Now he bought them. Stylish glasses graced his face. New clothes emerged from the closet. He joined a health club saying, "You need to join, too. Get into shape."

He hadn't seen a doctor in years. Without provocation, he made an appointment. Once there, he boasted how many pounds he could bench press.

"A man of 60 has no business exerting excessive muscle and energy without first having a stress test," Dr. Martin Brauweiler cautioned.

The test stopped mid-stream. A blocked artery showed on the screen. Mike needed angioplasty.

"I can't," Mike retorted. "I'm going fishing in two weeks."

Doc agreed to wait and put him on nitroglycerin to increase blood flow to prevent heart attack and stroke.

I, too, was eager for his annual fishing trip. It would give me time to dismount the pins and needles I had balanced on for more than a year. Throughout our courtship and marriage, Mike's kindness, devotion, gentleness, and concern for me were paramount. I wallowed in his attention. In his arms, I was safe and loved. There was nothing he would not do for me. If we were shopping, and I admired something, whether it was jewelry, dishes, collectibles, clothes, or furniture, it showed up for my birthday or appeared under the Christmas tree. When Channel # 5 ran low, it spontaneously refilled.

In the background, I remembered my mother's caution, "What you love most about the man you marry, you will grow to hate."

Wise she was. Mike's attentiveness smoked and blazed into uncontrolled jealousy. I was his ultimate possession. He spoke and jested with men and women alike while I dared not speak to a man. I had never been unfaithful or given him cause for concern, but when I did as he did, unfounded suspicion sparked.

I had to be accountable for every spoken word and every minute not in his presence. His insecurity foiled our marriage. Distrust was rampant. Coupled with inappropriate sexual conduct and nasty behavior towards my mother, I scheduled an appointment with a divorce attorney.

Mike tracked every outing including my time to and from work. Therefore, I dared not see a lawyer until he left town. If I was ten minutes late, he accused me of having an affair. I vowed never to be a battered woman, physically or mentally, and I meant it. Nor would I subject my mother to abuse of any kind. If divorce was the only way out, I intended to take it, but would resort to counseling first.

I loved the Mike that was. I despised the monster now within him. Still, I would not abandon the man when he was faced with newly found heart issues. I'd discover my legal rights and stay by his side through his heart surgery. Then, demand counseling. For sure, I was not blameless—I was mean. I'd leave for work without saying a word, pretend not to hear him when he called, and ate at the stove before telling him dinner was ready. If his meal was cold, too bad. I no longer warmed it as I had done before.

Yet, something prompted me to want to salvage this mess of a marriage. In my heart, I knew Mike was a good husband. Not for me, but for some woman who could deliver his imprisoned soul and recover the Mike I loved.

Happy times...sharing birthdays with the grandkids.

CHAPTER 4

Time to Heal or Time to Run?

Mike packed his bags and gathered his gear for his annual Arkansas fishing trip with his brother Bob and friends, Steve and Dale. Packing two weeks before departure was the norm for always prompt, thorough, and ahead-of-his game Mike. I was a last-minute Lucy, making sure I did the laundry and put it away half an hour before any departure.

I drove this orderly man and Mom crazy, but they loved me anyway. They were sticklers for completing one project before beginning another. I was not. I thrived on anything new and challenging—multiple projects always in motion.

I would get home from work around 5:30. The plan was to eat and then leave for Joliet. I'd drive Mike to his brother's where he'd spend the night. Early the next morning, they would meet their buddies and depart for Bull Scholes, Arkansas.

I rode to work that morning with my friend Colleen. On the way home, she said she needed to make a detour by way of her doctor's office to pick up a prescription. My stomach somersaulted.

Knots made freakish visits to my gut and the slightest deviation from Mike's demanded routine, always pickled my intestines.

I wanted Mike's departure to be smooth, without confrontation. A week of fishing and rest would calm his anxiety and mine. Restore our lives.

During all of this, it never occurred to me I should pray. I was strong, relied on myself. Years earlier, I battled a major Lupus flare. If I could handle Lupus, I could handle anything.

Colleen entered the doctor's office. I waited in the car. Forty minutes later, she emerged. Though near frantic, I said nothing as it was my problem, not hers. We couldn't avoid the delay as a hospital emergency detained the doctor. We didn't have cell phones, and I didn't consider using the doctor's phone to call home. Besides, it didn't matter how late I was—five minutes or forty. Either made Mike equally ballistic, even if I called. No excuse, short of my death, would be enough and I am not sure even death would suffice. It would be what it would be. I could change nothing.

I recalled a night a few months earlier when I was caught in a blinding downpour—late returning from an eye appointment. The optician said she found something questionable in her exam and suggested I see a doctor at once. "I hope it's not a brain tumor," she said.

Frantic and bewildered, I faced the drive home unable to see center lines, the road's edge, or cars ahead of me. I pulled off the highway numerous times hoping the rain would stop. I longed to be home in Mike's arms where he would reassure me, "All will be well. We will get through this together." Instead, he accused me of being with another man. He verbally badgered me for hours and demanded an explanation—other than the rain.

I never told him what the technician feared. He didn't deserve an explanation! An eye specialist found early budding cataracts.

I was correct. Accusations flew the minute I walked in the door. "What was I doing? Where had I been? Who was I with? What was his name? How could I be so inconsiderate and make him late? Did I not understand how important this was?"

"Colleen drove. I was at her mercy. It was a necessary stop. I don't control doctors or hospitals. I'm good, but not that good. Besides, what difference does it make what time you get to Joliet as long as it's before morning?"

"You're selfish and inconsiderate. Why did I marry you?

You can't be trusted. I don't trust you!" Irrational and excited, he stormed slinging his arms like a fish flapping to get into water.

One of my grandmother's favorite sayings was, "If you hang a man long enough, he'll get used to it." I wondered if I would live long enough to "get used to this."

The entire forty-mile trip from Lake Holiday to Joliet had him ranting, raving, screaming, and bashing the dashboard. Mike never behaved like this. I wanted this man out of my life for much longer than a week. I was furious and fed up with this obnoxious life. Mike had never been physical with me, but this behavior was leading to deadly. I knew it.

I didn't talk on the ride to Joliet. The slightest retort and he might grab the wheel and stir me into traffic. It relieved me to drop him off and be rid of him.

On the way home, I sank emotionally into deep waters. Weights entrapped my ankles. Thoughts became vocal, "Breathe deep, Mary Ellen. He will be out of your life soon. In his absence, you'll see the divorce attorney to learn your rights. I want a divorce and ALL his money. I deserve it."

When Mike was tranquil and seemingly reasonable, he'd suggest we sell everything and move to Sierra Vista, AZ, near his friends Pat and Gene Carpentier. "You're too close to your kids and your mom. We need to get away—just the two of us."

Crazy talk. Why would we move away from family and friends—especially while Mom was alive? I was in my 50s and Mike barely 60. Retirement in a warm climate was for our seventies when the grandkids were in college and didn't have time for us. We agreed on this. Commitment to parents and grandkids was a priority. When did it depart? And why, after five years, would he give up his dream of a lake home? It was always, "just the two of us." And what happened to his relationship with Mom?

When we first moved to the lake, the three of us, Mike, Mom, and I rode to church together on Sundays. Mike and Mom in the front seat with me in the back. To and from church, the two joined forces and recited litanies of what I did, did not do, and should have done the previous week. They were one on this mission. It never failed.

Finally, I had enough of their lectures and told them we would go to church together in different cars if they didn't stop weekly homilies.

Not understanding, I explained the two of them could continue to ride to church together and I would drive separate to avoid their sermons, but I would still sit with them in church.

Mike rolled his eyes and Mom apologized. "I'm sorry we do this to you. It's the only time you sit still and we have you captive."

I suggested they make a list of things they wanted me to address and I would complete them as time permitted.

The two melded perfectly until a year ago when Mike began to ignore Mom. I became his priority—his personal property. ME … just ME. One-hundred-fifty percent of ME. One-hundred percent of the time, day, night, and every second in-between. He commanded my constant presence either to make love or verbally mistreat me. Hot/cold, Jekyll/Hyde. Thankfully, he often slept in the living room chair. When he entered our bed, I'd pretend to sleep. Make-believe was usually futile. My only reprieve was when he left for a meeting or shopping, or when we had company. He was nice to others.

Why not me and Mom?

I'm suffocating. I gasp for air. I can't tell one day from another. If time passes, I have no awareness of the hours, minutes, or days. My thinking is disjointed. I'm a marionette on strings. Whose puppet, am I?

One Sunday, "just the two of us" went for chicken at a road-side Mendota restaurant. We laughed and had fun; thoroughly enjoyed each other's company. The Mike I married was back.

"See how nice things can be when there's 'just the two of us.' Let's sell everything and go to Arizona," he said.

When he was 'out-of-reach,' he'd fume and say, "I'm cashing in the investments, moving without you, and taking our refrigerator with me."

Yes, he said, "refrigerator."

The refrigerator comment left me confused. His brain was on holiday. The man was nuts! Baffled and exhausted, I needed to see a lawyer.

I vomited words on the attorney, "Mike tried to kill us on that Fox River drive, his increasing anger, my fear of sexual advances towards others in my absence—my mother. I dare not leave her or my grandchildren alone with him."

The conference ran longer than the free hour. Yet, the lawyer refused payment. Instead, he urged me to file for divorce. Serve Mike with papers the minute he returned from Arkansas.

"Mike's entire 401K is in his name; payable to you only upon his death. Legally, he can take the entire amount, skip town, and leave you with only half the house and any other investments you share. If you file now, it will freeze assets and we can negotiate your deserved portion."

"I can't do it. Something's amiss." I explained, "Fifteen years earlier, Lupus, a debilitating autoimmune disease, left me incapable of doing anything. This man nursed me for six months. I did not think I would survive—did not want to live. I was helpless. He dealt with an unspeakable situation and never once complained. How is it I cannot endure this? I have to give him a chance.

"During my illness, Mike was home-bound on crutches with a broken leg. Swallowing all pride, he bathed and fed me, even washed excrement from my body. I cannot turn on him. I can't, but I'm angry and I don't want half of everything. I want it ALL. I can't divorce him. I can't do it ... yet."

"Domestic violence, verbal and physical, is epidemic. Nine out of ten women who experience what you have and leave this office without filing, never get a divorce. They return to suffer silently and endure more abuse."

"I am the one in ten. I will not be abused. I will call and keep you informed. I will not live in an abusive marriage any longer. A year is a year too long."

I had worked for Henry Pratt Company through a temp agency for four years and turned in my resignation two weeks earlier saying, "I need to salvage my marriage." My last day would be the day before Mike would return from Arkansas.

During my illness, what the Bible refers to as "sins of the father" surfaced. While outsiders, friends, co-workers, nieces, and nephews thought Mike walked on water, his children and I saw his flip side.

Years before Monster took root, he had come to my bedside as I battled Lupus. He wanted to fly me to Mayo Brothers Hospital. It was then he verbalized his failures.

"I'm losing you. I can't let you go. You hold our family together. I don't know our children. I can't even remember their birth dates. I know Michael's falls three days before yours, but the girls? Both are 20 somethings in March and May. I never get them straight. Without you, there is no family. You can't die! I need you—they need you."

Mike like his father before him, failed to establish a personal relationship with his children. "That's your job," he'd say. "Mine is to discipline and be the provider."

I begged him to become involved in the kid's activities and he continued to be a workaholic and avoid intimacy with his children. History repeated itself. The father did not know his children.

He was a far better grandfather than he was a father. Perhaps he recognized "the sins of the father."

"Just the two of us"

CHAPTER 5

Welcome Home

Expecting wonderful changes in both of us, I dropped his car off in Joliet, so he could drive himself back to Lake Holiday. I also cut our gigantic hillside lawn with his walk-behind mower. Mike refused to buy a rider. It wouldn't make perfect rows.

Our lives and our marriage would renew.

Mike entered the house, rejected my advance, said nary a word, changed his clothes, and walked towards the door saying, "I'm mowing the lawn."

Demure and teary-eyed, I sputtered, "I mowed this morning. I thought you'd be pleased."

"Yes, but you didn't do it right!"

His criticism burnt. Moved me to furry. I had spent hours, sweating and sore, heaving his stubborn machinery up and down that blasted hill. But the anger dissipated as quickly as it blazed.

I wanted to be angry. I tried to scream but couldn't. I was infuriated with myself. No longer was I in control of my marriage or my emotions. I choked on self-hatred. Weak rivulets of water smoked my eyes.

"It's not done right. Go! Get out of my way," he ordered with a push.

I moved. Mom within ear-shot went to her room. Minutes later, Bob's wife Marge called.

"Did Mike make it home?" she asked chipperly. "When he got out of the car here, he didn't seem to comprehend where he was or who I was. He spoke gibberish. I couldn't understand him. Is he okay?"

She rattled on. I listened.

"The guys said he wasn't the same on the trip, had a lot of headaches, and seemed confused. Mike said it was the meds he was taking for his heart."

I thanked Marge for her concern but wondered why on earth they had let him drive forty miles home in "that" condition. Nothing computed.

"Did Mike drink in excess on the trip?" I asked.

"Let me ask Bob" she said pausing to question. "Bob says, 'Mike didn't drink a lot'."

I didn't believe it. He likely drank in secret. Then again, maybe the meds messed him up. Combine drugs and martinis, even a few martinis, and who knew what might have happened. He may have unwittingly blown his mind.

The next day was Mother's Day. Communication, even three-word sentences, did not happen. Mike left early for church while Mom watched services on television. I drove to church alone. If anything could move Mike, surely God's presence in a place of worship would.

Standing in the back of church, I scanned the pews. He always sat near the front. Today, he occupied the second to last row, alone. I entered his pew, sat beside him, and placed my warm hand over his. He remained still. Then, he withdrew and turned. Crushed, tears freely flowed. I felt grateful to be in the back of church where inquisitive eyes could not witness his rejection and my plaguing pain. When we returned home, all wrath surfaced. Our house, once again, became a fist-less boxing ring. Happy Mother's Day.

In all the years of marriage, Mike never entered my presence without speaking and he never passed without caressing my shoulder, kissing my neck, or hugging. It was just something he did. I loved it. He was consistent; never failed. Now, he had nothing kind to say nor did he stroke me unless he wanted sex which seemed continual. He did not acknowledge my presence if he could avoid it unless the bedroom was on his mind. When he barked orders, I barked back. If he asked for water, I told him to get off his butt and get it himself. When he suggested I close the drapes, I didn't. I let the sun's glare bounce off the television screen hampering his view. I'm no man's footstool.

Amy and her eight-month-old daughter Hailey arrived for Mother's Day dinner. Her husband Mark had to work. Mike immediately transformed into the sweet, gentle grandfather they knew, while my ire detonated.

Amy cornered me in the bedroom. "You are extremely unfair and unkind. Dad's no saint, but you are plain hateful!"

I WAS mean. I knew I was mean. But he deserved it! I apologized to Amy. Not to Mike. May 10, 1998, was the most awful Mother's Day of my life. I despised Mike. Loathed everything.

CHAPTER 6

The Pot Boils Over

The next morning, I laid in bed remembering his first touch at a high school dance. His hand firmly on my 14-year-old shoulder, heat registered to my dancing toes. "Can I cut in?" he asked. His smile carted me into his wings. Immediate lure on both ends. We twirled and circled the dance floor through several songs. Later, I told my friend, JoAnn, "I intend to marry him … or someone like him." She said I was nuts.

Mike was in college and I was a lowly high school freshman. He dropped me quickly when he discovered my age only to reappear from time to time during the following years. I was 18 when we married. He was 23. I finished high school and beauty school and worked a year at the Boston Store. Mike had graduated from Joliet Junior College with a major in business and completed two years in the US Army where he was a trained sharpshooter and cryptographer decoding messages. He also assembled and disassembled atomic weaponry—handled plutonium and uranium. When we married, he was an appliance salesman for Northern Illinois Gas Company in downtown Joliet.

Neither of us ignored or denied the magnetism. It never waned. Not even now. It was a new week. I would try again to reach his distant mind.

As we lay in bed, spring's dawn peeked through our bedroom window. I reached out to the man I no longer knew. I don't give up easily. His back turned toward me; his body hugged the edge of the bed. I rolled his way; cuddled close. No response to my advance. Yet, he did not reject me. Ah, progress.

I swallowed. My heart raced. Blood, a raging river in my veins. I licked my lips and began throatily, "Mike, I need you to listen. If you don't, you will die alone—an old man isolated from your family. You don't deserve that."

He did not recoil. He seemed to hear.

"You have ostracized our entire family and offended friends. You must get the heart surgery. Our marriage is a wreck. After your surgery, we need counseling to fix this. If you don't, I am out of here."

I paused. "Do you understand?"

He did not move for more than a minute before the sad mind behind distant eyes slowly propelled his legs over the bed's edge and put his feet on the floor. He nodded and walked to the bathroom devoid of expression.

Prepared for the worst, I waited, anxious for something, anything, to happen. I expected him to erupt with, "You're no Park Avenue princess. Not blameless. You're more like a swift kick in the ass! Don't fault me."

He did not react. Instead, he nonchalantly moseyed to the bathroom where he shaved, washed his hands and face, brushed his teeth, and combed his luscious, thick hair. I sat on the bed's edge and watched, intently waiting for him to return.

Mike, meticulously clean, always smelled pure and wholesome. I dearly loved that part of him. Now, his face changed to the façade of an empty safe, a guise of time unknown. Lost. Incredibly lost. He turned, walked my way, sat beside me on the bed, and tried to speak. His voice was shallow. At first, I could not discern his words.

An ominous force dominated the room. He began to cry—rare. An immediate rush of guilt swept over me, without reason.

"Oh Mike," I said, as I engulfed his shoulders, caressing him in assurance of my love, "I don't know what—"

He swung out of my arms. "Don't you touch me! I have something to say, and you WILL listen!" "Do NOT put your hands on me. Don't interrupt me. I've got to get this out … sometimes I don't know who you are! And that woman! That woman in the other room. What is she doing here?" His tone penetrated louder and deeper than his words.

"My God! ... OH MY GOD! That's my mom! You've had a stroke! Those meds were supposed to keep you from having a heart attack or stroke."

I took flight to the kitchen to phone Dr. Brauweiler while Mike screamed for me to come back—not to tell anyone.

"It isn't anyone's business!" His shouts followed me. He believed we should shroud our lives in secrecy. The doctor's office said to bring him right in.

When I returned to the bedroom, Mike calmed and only mildly protested. Once in the doctor's office, he was tranquil and expressionless. His face in no way reflected unexplainable anguish nor was he the unsettled man he had been at home.

Dr. Brauweiler leaned compassionately his way, "You may have a mental problem as I think you haven't accepted you have heart disease and need surgery."

"No. It's not here. It's not here," Mike repeated over and over while pounding his heart.

"It's here," he yelled with fists compressing his skull. "It's here! It's this medicine," he blurted flashing the bottle of pills at the doctor. "I'm not taking it anymore."

Doc explained the risks of not taking the nitroglycerin. Mike had none of it. "It's the medicine! Hear me!"

I took the pills from Mike's hand and dropped them into the wastebasket.

"Mike, you are in charge of your life. If you don't want to take the meds, you don't have to."

Truthfully, at that instant, I didn't care if he died. "Schedule the surgery ASAP Doc. We'll deal with whatever happens."

Brauweiler twisted in dismay. "This can't be done in an instant. It takes time. He needs the meds."

"No," I retorted, "Mike's in charge. Get it scheduled."

Mike seemed relieved someone finally listened, but the relief didn't last.

As we entered the car and I turned the key in the ignition, Mike placed his hand firmly over mine—a taunting move. I halted and looked him square on.

"You stop right there." His eyes were dangerously still. "Listen to me."

Like bullets shooting from a gun, he spoke. Slow, deep, and gruff, yet sickeningly calm, "I – Am – Going – To – End – It. I – Will - End - It - All."

Terror struck me silent. Thoughts jumped like a ball on a roulette wheel. I knew exactly what he meant. I withdrew my hand from under his, grabbed the keys, and flew out the car door as he fumed.

I raced hysterically into the patient-filled office and shrieked! "That man has guns. He will kill me and my mother! Then, he'll kill himself!"

I cannot imagine what patients and nurses thought. I didn't care. The in-control-of-life-wife became a raving lunatic. They were frozen in fear, mouths hung wide open as they grabbed arms on their chairs.

Would the deranged man enter and kill them as well? Dr. Brauweiler bolted from his new patient's side into the chaotic waiting room. "Take him to Mercy Center's emergency room in Aurora. They'll be expecting him. Do not go home for anything. Take him right there."

For more than a year, Mike's behavior had leaped between psychotic and calm. The uncertainty scared me ... the realm of expectations unknown.

Calm presided when I returned to the car. When he saw we weren't bound for home, he asked where we were headed.

"To the hospital."

"Good," he said, "I want to go home and get my things first."

He was lucid. I, stymied.

"I'll bring your clothes and toiletries later."

It surprised me Mike was content while I was riddled with fear, more than incensed, frantic—beyond my limits.

My world consisted of "my." My life, my husband, my house, my children, and my jobs. It left room for only one more thing—the capital I. I want, I need, I deserve. Mike ruefully invaded my and I.

Where was God in this mess? I thought I had a relationship with Him. But God was not part of our lives. Mike and I gave Him only an hour each Sunday. When we left church, we left Christ behind. Though devoted to church rules (most of them), God had no place in our real lives. God was in some box allocated to Him on Sunday. I didn't really know Him. I claimed to believe, yet I did not turn to serious prayer and praise. The prayer now said was delivered with no faith or hope attached. It was empty—like me.

The Gram gave her a toy roller coaster but Popee got all the hugs

CHAPTER 7

Tell Me, I Can Handle It

At Mercy Center, I sat on the other side of the room, as far from Mike as I could be. I wanted nothing to do with him. My life and my mother's life were the important issues. My head dropped into my cold hands. Masses of black, wet confetti swirled in my head. Intense and murky, slimy like algae. I couldn't move. Thick and foul. My breath felt rancid. Hope and faith were dead. Did this mess swirl in Mike's head?

Compassion could not survive in this arena. Finished with reason, immersed in a swamp of hate, resentment, and confusion, I fell limp. The stem of adrenaline that kept me going for months evaporated. I wilted. What happened to the world I regulated? Where was the God I knew?

A counselor spoke first with Mike and then with me. The hideous, revolting things we had kept behind closed doors charged from our mouths. Both of us regurgitated bitter bile, and they admitted Mike. I didn't say goodbye and didn't see what happened to him next. I didn't care.

Relieved to have him removed from sight, I did not return that night with his belongings as promised.

I gathered his things the next morning but was ill-prepared for what followed.

Mike was behind locked doors in a narrow, padded, starkly empty cell. A thin mattress lay on the bed. No sheets, pillows, or covers. No clothes. Only a hospital gown that barely covered his naked body. It horrified me.

Spirit moved in my heart. While I had slept soundly on a feather pillow, curled comfortably under a warm blanket, Mike existed nearly nude in a thickly padded cubicle. I should have known. Where else would they restrain a man who threatened suicide and murder?

"You've got to get me out of here. It's a prison. There are crazy people in here."

"Sorry friend, can't until they finish with tests."

I left, went home, and waited for the diagnosis giving no thought to what I would do with him when released. Hours later, neurosurgeon Dr. George Handley called.

"I need to speak with you. Can you be here within the next fifteen minutes?"

Dr. Handley's voice had gentle clarity—young, strong, and measured. Despite his urgency, there was an audible softness in his manner. I spoke no softness.

"No," I said as flippant as a teen blowing off a class assignment. "I am forty-five minutes away."

"I have a rash of surgeries ahead of me. It's imperative we speak immediately!"

I reiterated the distance between us. Callous and sharp, I added, "You'll just have to tell me over the phone. I can handle it."

"I do not do things like that," he insisted with shock apparent in his pitch. "I never do that."

"There's no choice. Unless you want to wait until tomorrow or maybe later in the week when you have more time," I snapped, recalling Mike's behavior the past year.

He paused. His voice lowered. "I really don't want to do this."

"Wait," I interjected, "I want to get my daughter Janet on the other line. I want to be sure I understand and misinterpret nothing."

Janet picked up the extension.

"There is no easy way to put this," he began. "I have conferred with seven neurosurgeons.

We all agree." He took deep breaths. "Your husband has a brain tumor called a Glioblastoma."

My feet slid sideways. I steadied on the counter's edge. Then, stumbled into a chair. My throat was raw. It bled disbelief.

He hesitated ... "I am very sorry. It's centered in the Broca and engulfs the frontal lobes which control personality." He stopped to give me seconds to absorb ... "Your husband has approximately three months to live."

"No, you're wrong!" I raged, instantly on my feet. "You have to be wrong! That's not possible! What else looks like a Glioblastoma!"

"Nothing. Nothing else resembles a Glio. Nothing. I AM truly sorry."

Every inch trembled. Water drained from my pores. I couldn't feel. I was beyond numb. "What's next? What treatment? Where can we go from here?" I rambled. "There has to be something we can do."

I hated ME. Hated every cruel word hurled, every thought wishing him dead, every bitter stare cast to pierce his heart. How wicked can a human be and not even care? Evil, bastard, Satan-filled. This was me, all me. Would I ever forgive myself? This was never to have happened. We had plans. I cannot survive without him. Can't anyone hear me!! This isn't happening. I won't let it happen. It isn't real. We planned to grow old together.

"Treatment? I can't advise you about that. Consult your primary or an oncologist."

"No! That's not fair!" I hurled loud words at the man! "You drop a death sentence and leave us to hang? No. No. NO! I need you to tell me what YOU would do if you or YOUR wife received the diagnosis of a Glioblastoma. What would YOU do?!"

Cornered, forced to answer, he swallowed. His Adam's apple likely bobbed up and down. I do not believe he had ever been verbally accosted like this before. I sought truth. No empty hopes. No lies.

"We have an unspoken rule between neurosurgeons: 'If any of us is ever diagnosed with a Glio, we do nothing. No surgery and no treatment. They only postpone the inevitable'." His voice trailed to a near whisper, "Palliative care only for pain."

He rested again. "When I saw the Glio, it resembled an octopus squeezing his brain. The brain—horrendously swollen. It's a wonder it didn't burst."

My mouth filled with phlegm. The clothes on my body were too small. Skin tightened ... and bloated, the way fingers do when coming in from dead winter's cold. Hot coals dumped on me, one, by one, by one. Then, tumbled in masses. I folded and waited for a bulldozer to follow. How could this happen? Barely 60, he never was sick. Life had just begun. He just retired. I had plans. We had plans.

I had screeched at Mike, called him names under my breath, tried to leave him. Mike—lost, confused, alone and dying.

Mary Ellen, outrageously senseless and cruel. I should have known. I should have known. I was the monster.

Dr. Handley went on, "Your husband will be on steroids. His condition will improve some, but only for a brief time. Take this opportunity to get your affairs in order and heal your relationship—if you can."

A breath out … I went silent before asking, "What will the end be like?"

"If you do nothing, he will simply sleep away. Once the tumor hits the brain stem, he will sleep. He will be relatively free of pain."

A deafening hush prevailed. Birds outside lost voice. Doctor Handley broke the silence, "I have a request … I watch this horrible thing happen to good, loving couples like you and your husband and I wonder how they get through it. I cannot begin to imagine. Will you keep in contact with me? Let me know? I need to understand how you survive this nightmare. Please."

I responded with little strength, "Yes." However, I would never complete that promise. I couldn't. Until now.

Janet and I fell into each other's arms. We spoke no words. No comfort nor hope to share. I went to Mom, a pillar of strength, a woman who shed no tears and confronted hurdles stoically straight on. This time, she too folded and droplets slipped down her walled cheeks.

I always thought I controlled my life. I only asked God for things I wanted. When life blustered, I implored Him to fix things—like Mike. I did not understand what His Word, the Bible, had to say on any subject. God-He-God was not in our marriage. I only thought He was. Now, we needed Him.

I called my other two children, Michael and Amy, following the diagnosis. Amy lived 40 minutes away in Minooka, IL, and Michael lived in Mesa, AZ.

Michael made flight reservations for the following day. He left his pool business in the hands of a friend and came home to care for his father. His wife and son stayed in AZ. He would stay throughout the illness plus an additional six weeks after his father's death.

The Aschenbrenner family poses for a family photo in June 1998. L to R: Mary Ellen, Janet, Mike, Amy and Michael

CHAPTER 8

Hundred-Dollar Bills and Urine

The next morning, I arrived at the hospital and sat in the waiting room. The counselor who interviewed us the day before asked to speak with me.

A long, cool woman dressed in black, her demeanor spoke "bothered." It said, "I don't want to do this, it hurts, get it over with." She executed verdicts far too many times, but never mastered the art of decorative cosmetology–painting a smile while speaking consoling words. Void of personality, she displayed no soothing attributes.

Early morning, her office contained stacks of well-organized folders in neat rows on her polished desk, all ready to share. The room ... disciplined like she was. She fit the stereotype laid on spinster school teachers. I'd place bets she didn't have pets to foil her structured life that likely resembled a Bonsai.

Riddled with questions, I gushed, unhinged. "When she interviewed us, did she recognize it as a brain tumor? How could I have been naïve? Not have known? What should we do next? Will he have to be institutionalized? Is he dangerous to himself? Am I at risk? Did Mike know? Would they tell him–or should I?"

Her words replicated a sharp sickle. "Yes," she said. "I strongly suspected a brain tumor when Mike said his food tasted metallic. That symptom often points to brain disorders. It's even prevalent in epilepsy. Call your primary physician. Discuss options. In the meantime, get finances in order and speak with the family. You will need support for this journey."

I didn't like her, with her organized office and flawless appearance. Her desk was a myriad of 90-degree angles. Her hair, never frizzy. But she had answers and for the first time in my life, I craved a perfectionist attitude like Mike always carried. The sense of sureness, of absolute control. I wanted control. I wanted it badly.

She relayed: "The tumor, centered in the Broca, controls speech. That's why he often speaks in simple, three-letter words and short sentences, 'yes, no, do this, do that.' Its size entraps the frontal lobes explaining personality change."

Then, what I feared, "With the location of his tumor, he would or could be a danger to himself and others. Confiscate car keys. Get guns out of the house. Never turn your back. No, Mike hasn't been told. Do you want to tell him or do you want staff to tell him?"

She handed me lists of doctors, medical facilities, and institutions trained to handle cases like ours.

I decided I would tell Mike. I would be the one to say, "I am sorry for how I've behaved. I will be at your side all the way."

Those words, enormously simple—inadequate considering how I acted. They would sound hollow and heartless following the venom I spewed. Yet, I would beg forgiveness and speak them in a few moments with all my heart.

At the psych ward, a nurse flagged my attention. "I need to give you Mike's belongings and oh yes, there's the matter of hundred-dollar bills. Are you aware, Mike stuffed hundred-dollar bills under the lining of his shoes? He tried to give them to the nurses and attendants. He also folded hundreds in his trench coat pockets and seams."

I reckoned he attempted to bribe the staff to release him from his padded cell.

She suggested I check the house for hidden money and review checking and savings accounts. "Make sure he hasn't passed funds to others without your knowledge."

A smile slid over me–the first in many, many months. It was just like Mike to give to others. I so, so loved THAT man!! Mike lay on a barren bed. He smiled. Happy to see me. “I had a healthy b.m. and a decent amount of urine this morning,” he boasted. “I don’t think anything is wrong with me. I’m ready to go home.”

B.M.? Urine? Dying and concerned about elimination? I wondered—should I chuckle or would a cry be more fitting?

“Mike, before you dress for home, I need you to listen very carefully. Like the doctor said, ‘There is no easy way to tell you this’. I will do the best I can.”

I drew close, leaving no space between us to sway his attention. Yesterday’s Bay Rum lotion still fresh on his body, clean burst through panic in his eyes. He wanted nothing more than to get out of that place. He did not want me to speak. He wanted to go home where he would be safe from others in this asylum, a place where he could have his clothes, shoes, lotions, bed, and hundred-dollar bills.

“No,” I insisted. “Look at me with your green eyes. Tell me you will understand what I am about to tell you.”

Our eyes met. I searched for signs of understanding behind the fog.

“First off, I have been mean and cruel. I am eternally sorry.” I said the words with more compassion than I had ever owned.

Mike stared at the sterile floor. His eyes shifted side to side.

"Look at me." I breathed softly as I laid hands on his flawless face. "I love you intensely … with all of my heart. I will never leave you. I will always be at your side. Nothing, NOTHING will ever separate us. You are not responsible for the pain I have endured and I ask forgiveness for the hurt I have inflicted on you."

His eyes depleted. They said nothing … as though a blank tape played in his recorder. His attention reached no further than the short sentences he spoke, "yes, no, stop, go."

How on earth would I find words to cross his resilient brain barrier?

Without thought, prayer crossed my lips. "God give me wisdom. Put simple words in my mouth. Allow me to speak clearly. Bring understanding to this man who must confront his end. Empower us both."

But Mike's eyes did not see and his ears did not hear. Like a little child, he half nodded and pulled away. I cupped his chin like a mother does her child. It rested in my quaking hand, inches from my wretched, miserable face. Again, I urged, "Look at me. I will be with you to the end. I will never leave you."

My words flew about as though guided by propellers. Could he comprehend even a snippet?

I spoke again, "The doctors found something very serious. You have an inoperable brain tumor."

My words ended allowing him to inhale his death sentence.

He was pale, as though embalmed, as white as the bed he lay on. He gasped. The hush, a helpless hoar, an obnoxious rumble of inaudible sound—as profane as the Monster within.

"How long do I have?"

"A few months."

He dressed neatly and methodically. We left the hospital. The trip home lingered. It lacked conversation as we were solo in our thoughts. He went straight to the bedroom. I followed, sinking passionately into his commanding arms. Frantic, we tore at each other's clothes; zealously kissing. The fervor and intensity beyond premier. Every movement filled with relentless passion. Our bodies craved more and more. Our desire to love, to complete each other, not repeatable. Never before had the obsession, the hunger for oneness, and the expression of fidelity devoured us. We consumed each other.

Sting or sweetness? Pure or pervasive? Clear and cunning or futile and final? Regardless, we wanted more. We wanted the life Monster would cheat us of.

I was grateful for the steroids. Monster was the devil, but for those brief moments in the bedroom, the devil slept and I had my husband. For a few weeks, he once again spoke in complete sentences.

Meanwhile, Mom deferred to her room. For the rest of Mike's life, she would never stay in the same room with him.

"I can't deal with it," she said. "When your Dad died at 54 from strokes, I prayed none of my children would watch anyone lose their mind. Now, this ..."

I laid on the sofa less than an hour after making love that day and reached for Mike's hand as he sat next to me in the recliner. We smiled indulgently. Tears welled. The TV blared, but neither of us took particular interest. Words were not needed to express our love, our trust, our oneness ... I thought.

The magic of those bedroom moments turned into irony minutes later as Mike spoke over the TV, "I have something to ask you. Will you tell me the truth?"

Sweet and tender in his request, I melted. "Of course, I will. You can ask me anything. I will never lie to you." I expected he would question his diagnosis.

He articulated words and didn't scramble a single syllable. "Have you ever noticed how different our children look? They all look so different."

I nodded, wondering where his mind traveled to conjure those thoughts and assemble such statements.

"Who are their fathers?"

My throat locked. "NO!" I gasped. His mind again kidnapped.

"No?" he said. "You shake your head, 'No.' You won't tell me? You won't tell me who their fathers are! You promised!"

A sickened expression befell his face. My jaw shuddered. My head bobbed insisting, "NO, you can't possibly question my fidelity after what we just shared." Shards. My heart cracked into thousands of shards."No ... NO ... you can't possibly think ..."

"You won't tell me. You won't tell me." My silence crushed him; his heart again destroyed.

I denied his request. I had promised—promised to tell him anything and all I could do was shake my head, "NO."

Devastated, but not angry, he drifted back into darkness. No words could heal his deranged fantasy. Further denial or attempt to enlighten would only deepen those fabricated gashes. His gaze, crazed.

Would this terror never end? When moments of saneness or warmth ensue, would they forever be assailed? When he dies, will this be all I remember of the man I treasure?

At moments like these, I feel dead. Maybe feeling lifeless is good. I don't think or try to understand. I remind myself over and over again, Mike is faultless. It is not he who says and does these things. He has become paranoid and schizophrenic.

Mike never brought his children's paternity up again, but he told me he saw me have sex in the garage. His narrative was graphic ... I had sex with a muffler.

Another time, he did not want me to go to a meeting. "I forbid you to go," he insisted. Another single-sided screaming match. No more fighting on my end as he no longer forgave anything—real or imagined.

I left without comment. As I walked out the door, he said to Mom, "He got her. He got her again." What images did his psychotic brain conjure?

Some weeks later, I shared his hypersexuality with his oncologist. "I can't trust him out of my sight and I worry about Mom. His friends want to take him to lunch and union meetings. My goal is to protect his dignity."

"This is normal for the location of his tumor. This is not your husband. If things get too out-of-control, we'll increase the meds."

Things were out-of-control. And, so we medicated. I prefer to think Mike never acted on his fantasies as he remained a faithful husband prior to this malady. But I am left to wonder what may have transpired during the year or two preceding Monster's discovery. It no longer matters. Be kind. Don't tell me.

A few weeks later, Mike became devastated again. "I can't 'do it' anymore." The meaning, more than clear. He couldn't perform in the bedroom. "You need to find someone," he said. "It's okay with me, but I want him to be good to you. Bring him home. I want to meet him."

I thought I had heard everything and nothing could shock me. The jealous husband desires for me to bring another man into our bed. He intends to make the gigolo pass inspection and give him an approval rating. Unreal!

"No," I said. "Not going to happen."

"It's necessary," he insisted. "Please."

CHAPTER 9

Putting Affairs in Order

In the days that followed, Mike and I broke the news to friends and family. Mike became furious each time I relayed information on his brain tumor, symptoms, and therapy. He wanted to tell everyone himself. Yet, he often could not get the words out or convey information correctly. The phone rang incessantly. I repeated the sad details over and over—upsetting Mike each time I shared his story. When he told it, it did not upset him.

In desperation and to avoid arguments, I had a second line installed in the basement. When friends called and asked about Mike, I'd say, "If you call (insert number) you can get that information and please tell others about the number. Mike was clueless and never questioned. The new line's ringer was off and a message gave updates on Mike's condition without Mike having to hear it. (Dated phone messages appear throughout the book.) The home line remained intact.

I updated Mike's information on the recording every few days when possible, trying to begin with a positive note. As time went on, finding anything upbeat became difficult. I found the second phone line to be a godsend and suggested it to others who faced similar situations. Some said, "Those messages were depressing. I would never do that." I wondered why anyone would call the alternate line if it depressed them. I suspect they wanted to hear only good news. I didn't have any.

> **(Phone Message)** *May 31: "Many beautiful cards and messages have come our way. People are kind and thoughtful, asking how they can help. Although Mike's short-term memory is nearly nonexistent and his sight fails, he speaks lovingly and often of you, his family and friends, and he remains physically active."*

There were some "almost" sane moments … minutes when he didn't travel to regions unknown. They flashed when Monster slept. Or, at least it comforts me to remember them that way. One evening we sat together on our deck as a sailboat drifted by. The silence was long. The wind sang like a melodious chorus.

"I want you to do something for me."

"Anything," I said. "Just tell me and your wish is my command," I smiled.

"When I don't recognize anyone anymore, I want you to put me away someplace."

"Sorry friend, not gonna happen." I laughed light-heartedly.

"Then, I want you to help me die."

"Really?" I said attempting to turn this into something far less staid. "You want me to help you die and then, I go to prison? You want that for me?" I continued to smile hoping he'd grin and say he was being playful.

"You're a smart woman. You could do it. No one would be the wiser. You can do it," he assured. He was serious.

"Mike, when it's time, I promise to let you go. You'd do he same for me."

"Like hell, I would!" he exploded. "I'd keep you forever! And when I am gone, I want you to care for others who are helpless like me. You're good at it. You can make lots of money."

Oh, brother, I thought. Just what I want to do for the rest of my life—care for people who are ill, losing their minds, and dying. Isn't that dandy!

"Sorry," I said. "Never. Never-ever gonna do that! I've done my time."

Mike meant he would keep me forever. He'd keep me alive by any means available. Many times, we discussed quality of life versus quantity and claimed to be of one mind on end-of-life directives. We were not.

We both had said, "No feeding tubes. No life support when we were brain dead or could not return to functional."

Despite our vows, he would resuscitate me. His values, our values, were no longer his. They were Monster's. If the situation was reversed, he would foil my directives and resuscitate me—even if I was beyond dead.

I gasped. Tried to stay tranquil but irritation crept up my spine. "Mike," I snarled, "I have never called anyone a 'son of a bitch' in my entire life. But, if you would keep me alive when I was a vegetable and recognized no one, then you are a son-of-a-bitch and God is just by taking you first!"

Neither of us was angry, but I sure was loud! I suppose I should have realized sooner that life support was one-sided and he would keep me alive at all cost.

When my Lupus flared years back, he gave no thought to his own condition at the time—a broken leg, crutches, lack of employment, and his own excruciating pain. He begged to take me to Mayo Clinic.

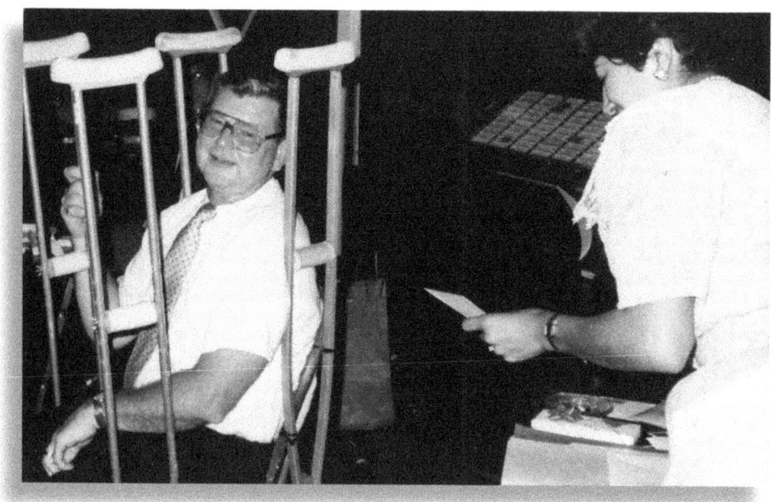

As Mike prepared to relocate to G.O. Headquarters, his Joliet co-workers created a "Throne of Crutches" at his going away party.

I would honor his wishes even if he wouldn't have honored mine.

Explaining to friends and family about the hyper-sexuality became rote. One more thing I had to do. Close my eyes and do it. I don't think they believed me as when I warned them to watch him every second–especially around women—they "yeah yeahed" and assured me,"Mike would never." They were correct, Mike would never. But this wasn't Mike.

I only allowed him to go to one union meeting without me as I would permit no one to besmirch his name nor any situation to present itself that would tarnish this moral man. I would see to it, the vulgarity of the monster within, stayed within.

A month into the illness, Michael's wife Alice and their infant son David followed to Illinois. They sacrificed beyond expectations. Without my son's presence, I would not have been able to care for Mike at home as my mother's safety and my own became compromised.

Life, now tenuous, had lost purpose. I told Alice; a brain tumor was the most horrendous diagnosis one could have with one exception ... Alzheimer's. Alzheimer's would be the same but would loiter for years, endlessly erasing Mike by bits and pieces. This, I prayed, would be quick.

I had no idea how long three and a half months of quick would be.

With Mike on steroids and somewhat clear-headed, we settled financial affairs and updated wills. Mike spoke matter-of-factly about funeral arrangements. "I've been thinking maybe we should do what your Mom and Dad did—donate our bodies to medical research. How do you feel about that?" he asked. I agreed.

Mike did not care about funeral details nor did he dictate where he wanted his ashes scattered or buried. As there would be no body, there would be no wake, only a memorial service. We signed the donor papers and never discussed it again. We would donate our entire bodies to medical science through the Illinois Anatomical Society. They would return our ashes three to six months later for burial at the location of our choosing.

The following Sunday, we attended Mass. He wanted to speak with the priest after service to tell him about the tumor and that he was going to die. Again, he wanted to do this himself. He also wanted to receive the Last Sacrament "for the dying."

"Mike, they've changed the sacrament's name to the Sacrament for the Sick"

Mike wouldn't hear of it, "I'm dying. I'm not sick!"

After the service, Mike spoke with the priest and received the Sacrament of the "Dying." I then asked the priest if we could renew our vows as I wanted to reassure Mike, it would be "death till us part—I would never leave him, no matter how bad things might get."

"Why not say your vows another time when all your family can be present to celebrate with you?" the priest suggested. Mike's white complexion toasted. He huffed and sputtered, left in a tizzy, tore out of the church, threw open the car door, and vented.

"I can't believe you've forgotten your vows. I won't stand for it! None of it! You better remember and remember them fast! And, if you can't, you go and say them again. I remember mine. The very idea! I will not put up with it for one minute!"

Wow! A complete paragraph without sputtered words.

We did not renew our vows. Mike remembered his, and I immediately remembered mine.

He also wanted to tell our neighbors, but I felt it unfair to leave them defenseless, searching for words. I told them in advance and asked them to act surprised when Mike relayed the information.

Throughout Mike's illness, they supported us in countless ways. Kay Smith, the owner of several spas, offered massages and services to our family. They provided much-needed respite.

Meanwhile, the phone rang off the hook. Everyone had an opinion. "I can't believe you aren't fighting this—not doing something," repeated over and over. Well-intentioned callers offered advice urging us to seek treatment and cure.

Several sent lists of experimental studies conducted at Chicago and out-of-state hospitals. Unwisely, I let Mike speak with some of these well-meaning friends who shared opinions. I still had not accepted Mike could not reason—at least a little. My hope was for Mike to have moments of clarity and let him make as many decisions as possible. By the weekend, Mike, restless and often reckless, insisted on a second opinion. I called Dr. Handley who gave the original diagnosis and asked for guidance.

"I suppose you can get a second opinion. You are entitled, but I conferred with seven neurologists. There is barely one chance in hundreds or thousands he could have a brain infection. And, he doesn't. It's an inoperable tumor," Dr. Handley said.

"The doctors gave me a death sentence. I have nothing to lose. I'm having a second opinion," Mike blurted commanding immediate charge.

Friends recommended a well-known Chicago hospital. Our entire family gathered for support as did his oldest brother Joe. To my surprise, our financial advisor Mike Lukas who guided us through Mike's retirement process also showed for the biopsy.

"I want to be here," Mike said. "When someone trusts you with their life savings as your Mike has, a special bond forms. Your Mike was responsible for my going to NICOR to present retirement options to employees. We have a relationship. I need to be here."

We scheduled family photos immediately following the initial diagnosis. It was a wise decision as once he had the biopsy, went on steroids, and began treatments his looks changed. In three weeks' time, Mike was barely recognizable.

They shaved Mike's head and drilled a hole. He did not flinch, "Sorry you have to see me bald," he said.

"I loved your silvered, wavy, brown hair, but bald is beautiful."

The biopsy confirmed "cancer." However, the official diagnosis of a Glio was negated. The new diagnosis was Anaplastic Astrocytoma, a far less virulent brain tumor than a Glio.

"That means, you can cure me!" Mike screamed with his infectious laugh.

"No," the doctor said. "It only means you have more time. Your tumor is inoperable, but it is slow growing." He repeated ... "Slow-growing ..."

"Will I see Christmas?"

"Oh yes! This is June. With chemo and radiation, you definitely will see Christmas! You've got at least a year."

The other doctors bobbed heads in unison. Ecstatic. Thrilled—as if they could cure Mike.

To me, they injected poison.

"What do you mean!" I blurted. "You intend to prolong the inevitable and cause more pain with chemo and radiation when you cannot cure him? What kind of life are you giving him!" I yelled. "Why would you do this? This is not what Mike said he wanted before all this happened!"

Mike and I had discussed his own mother's dementia and agreed neither of us wanted to live in that condition. These doctors offered remedies to extend the dementia Mike feared and despised. It would add months of pain and suffering.

"We deal with insanity and you want to increase his time? You can't give him back his mind!"

I should have shut my mouth, but didn't.

The doctor replaced his wide grin with professional tenderness, "You are correct. I can't give him something he doesn't already have, but I can give him time. It's apparent, the two of you have unresolved issues."

"I'll take it!" Mike jumped to his feet, danced, and shouted, "I'll see Christmas!" His excitement reverberated through walls. I had never seen him so joyous.

On the way home, our son Michael sat beside me in the car as having the unpredictable father next to the driver would be unwise. This also left Michael free to buffer potential tantrums. We dared not trust.

Tantrums were frequent.

Mike's words leaving the hospital were harsh, critical of my thoughtless comments to the doctor. Once in the car and the motor started, he detonated. Level-headed Michael attempted to restrain and quiet his father. Michael tranquilly said, "Dad you need to calm yourself."

I didn't look back at Mike or offer to help Michael. I knew my words would further inflame the situation. My eyes never strayed from the road. Michael wasn't his Dad's favorite person these days.

"Pull over, Mom. Pull off the road."

He repeated, "Dad, you need to calm yourself."

"I want out of here," Mike burst thrashing about in the back seat while condemning us to hell.

Michael placidly opened his father's door to facilitate his father's escape. Mike flung arms wildly at his son and fled through the open door into the busy Chicago avenue. His stance was bold; arrogance stamped all over him. He lambasted us and thrashed his arms uncontrollably.

Michael said his mind burst like fireworks. "I love my Dad. I love my Mom. My Dad is still in there, but he is not in control. To protect him and everyone else, I need to make wise decisions.

"Dad will not be here next year. I must make sure there is still a family left when this is over. I will protect my family with my life and I will protect my Dad. But I must restrain him. He is strong. If he were behind me when I was driving and 'went off' what would have happened?"

Michael seemed calm and appeared to know what he was doing. He later testified, "I wasn't in control and didn't know what I was doing."

However, Michael's training at the Maricopa Sheriff's Department automatically engaged. "I repeated to myself what I learned in training … diffuse … isolate … subdue … and, I prayed, God please, don't make this one of those situations. You've let him out safely … isolate … give him time … seek to diffuse. Respond to Dad as you would to a potentially violent inmate … Geesh??? Is this for real?"

"Dad, if you can remain calm until we get home, we can continue with the trip and get you home. … Here's a second option: We can go to a nearby hotel until things resolve … but then, you won't be home or have your 'stuff.' Wouldn't you want to have a steak for dinner? (Here's a full-grown man and I'm trying to convince him to eat his broccoli!)

"When you compose yourself—the whole way, we can try this again."

Michael tried this approach three or four times before his father could assure him, he could be in control and before Michael believed him.

Michael opened the car door for his father to reenter. Mike cooperated fully. What a blessing!

Fearful of a repeat performance, I headed back to the hospital's emergency room where doctors sedated Mike and counseled me. I was manic and likely should have been medicated, too. They admitted Mike. Michael and I drove home alone.

I never understood why so many of Mike's episodes took place in the car. He had never been claustrophobic. Perhaps it was a double deadbolt. First, locked out of his mind, and then, locked into the family vehicle.

During the days that followed, Michael said he reviewed the situation many times.

"Dad thinks every one of us is his enemy. However, when it comes to the safety of everyone else, he is the only one at risk. I see my father as a threat to my family. He must understand, I am also a threat, a big threat—and I will tolerate nothing that brings harm to anyone."

Michael said other thoughts rolled, "I also thought: "What must that do to a man? Sequestered in his own brain, the tumor isolates him from us. As the isolation grows, anger and resentment towards us increases.

"I love my dad but there is no way for him to EVER have an assurance of my love again. When he leaves this world, his seclusion will be complete. God, what an awful way to go. He will hate me when he dies. God, he will despise me but he has to fear me for the sake of everyone else. He has to see that I will tolerate nothing less or he won't die at home. He would have to exist elsewhere. There is no option ... for him ... for the family. This is my lot. There is no good outcome. Just the best of the worst. Pain for all. I entitle the man to live as long as he wants. I am committed. I will do this as long as necessary."

A kiss is just a kiss but love endures

CHAPTER 10

Struggles for Control

I called the hospital the next day to check on Mike.

"I'm sorry," the staff nurse said. "When we admitted him, we asked whom we should share his information with and your husband said, 'No one. I have no one.' Sorry ma'am, I cannot give you information on the patient."

I tapped the "off" button and lobbed the handset across the room. My exhausted, tormented self flopped onto the bed where I wailed myself unconscious.

Why can't I get myself under control? The poor man is lost; thinks no one loves him or wants him. He is desperately alone, trapped in a Mid-summer Night's Dream. In his own words, he said, "I have no one."

How is it, I am cruel and haven't control over emotions? Words roll freely and carelessly from my lips. Mike's assailant is himself. Must I always feed his feverish frenzy?

I laid lifeless, close to comatose from mental and physical exhaustion for at least an hour. When I awoke,

I gathered composure and the shreds from around the room before calling Dr. Brauweiler. I asked him to contact the hospital and have Mike released to our care. I also asked him if the angioplasty for his heart blockage would proceed.

"No," he said, "Mike would be fortunate if the heart takes him."

We brought Mike home without incident and began what was to be the new norm—gaggles and droves of foreign footsteps leading to the day of Monster's departure. I asked God to allow the heart blockage discovered months earlier to take Mike's life quickly. End this nightmare.

> **(Phone Message)** *June 1: "The initial biopsy report is carcinoma—no surprise. Final, detailed radiological reports are due the end of the week. Today, he is blacktopping the drive. He says he's getting the place ready for me to sell. I hate to break it to him, but I intend to live here forever. Mike worked hard for us to have this dream property on a lake. I'll NEVER leave."*

We took Mike's car keys and guns as told. We gave the guns to Janet for safekeeping. They will go to Michael. Relinquishing the guns and keys has turned into major issues just as my not selling the house has. I'd like to think better times lie ahead as he shines when guests arrive. Mike is blessed with innumerable friends who take him places. I continue to schedule as many visits with family and friends as possible as when they visit, he is civil—normal behavior for someone with a brain tumor like his, but it makes things difficult.

> **(Phone Message)** *June 7: "On his way to church, Mike had difficulty walking. When I noticed, he tried to cover it up and said, 'Sometimes, I have a little trouble walking but once I get going, I'm okay.' He seems determined not to be a burden."*

> **(Phone Message)** *June 15: "We had a doctor's appointment today to discuss treatments. The appointment went well. There are two options: chemo and radiation together to shrink the tumor and then, the use of the Gamma Knife, high-powered radiation concentrated on the tumor, followed by another dose of radiation. A second option is to reverse the order. It will be the doctors' decision."*

While waiting to schedule the radiation, I received a call from another well-known hospital. A relative or friend likely called them and shared details of Mike's condition. "Would I bring Mike to Chicago to discuss details of promising procedures?"

I agreed to the conference but would not bring Mike as he jumped at every option presented and I did not want a repeat of the fiasco that happened at the previous hospital. It was not going to happen.

Two young doctors introduced several experimental treatments successful in prolonging lives of Glio and Astro patients. The stipulation for entry into the trials: The patient may not have had any chemo or radiation prior to entering the studies. They begged to enroll Mike.

I know they meant well and wanted to foster hope—a false hope I dared not have. They drooled over a young, healthy "prospect." My mouth chalked at their words, "He's so young and strong. Do you have any idea what this will mean to others down-the-road?"

I listened intently. Mike's excellent, overall health made him a perfect guinea pig. I read the admission forms where it explained surgery would be foremost. They admitted they could not eradicate "Monster."

I would have to sign documents saying, I realized it could leave Mike paralyzed, incontinent, and/or unable to speak or eat. But then again, perhaps not. By this time, I was hardened to empty promises for the fatally ill. Pie-in-the-sky cures for Glios and advanced Astros had reached the fate of wilted lettuce. There was no cure. Chemo, radiation, and surgery only prolong the inevitable—just as Dr. Handley said.

"Tell me," I said. "You remove as much of the tumor as you can and he cannot speak, walk, eat, or control body functions. That will be for the rest of his life. You say it will give him an extra year or maybe even two. That just makes Mike a vegetable for a year or two longer. This should excite me? Foster hope?"

"Oh, if that happens, we'd begin therapy at once. We'd reteach him to walk and communicate, but that may not even be necessary. If it is, you'd bring him in every day for therapy. We cover all your expenses," the beautiful, young, female neurologist urged. Her male cohort caught her eye and exuberantly agreed. Their heads nodded in unison. More bobbleheads.

"Interesting proposal," I said. "I can lift his helpless, 220-pound body into my car each morning, drive two hours in Chicago traffic and pray he doesn't have outbursts and kill us all so you teach a dying man to walk and talk for the sake of science. This is not something I can readily absorb. I will have to go home and discuss it with my children," I lied.

In reality, I knew I would not mention it to anyone. I also had radiation and the Gamma Knife to consider.

The Gamma Knife non-invasively treats a variety of brain diseases and disorders including malignant and benign brain tumors. It delivers precise beams of gamma radiation to small targets inside the brain at a single, fine focused point with 192 beams. It attacks the diseased tissue while sparing nearby healthy tissue from the radiation. The doctors said, the "knife" was bloodless, painless, and did not cause hair loss.

The hair loss statement—useless. Chemo and radiation that would follow would leave him bald, anyway. As wicked as Gamma Knife sounded, it didn't sound as vile as chemotherapy and surgery. They made nausea churn in my gut.

Oh yes, what did Hadley say? "Do nothing. It will end quick and quiet." Was that not what Mike, in his right mind, wanted? He longs to live but is this living? Mike says he's not afraid to die.

What am I doing except wasting valuable minutes with Mike before he no longer knows me? I will not meet with another doctor.

Mike wanted to combat the tumor in his skull and began radiation at Mercy Center in Aurora after Fathers' Day, a month after the diagnosis.

> **(Phone Message)** *June 20: "We celebrated Father's Day one day early at "R Place" in Morris. Mike loved being with his grandchildren. The gifts were perfect—his preferred choices: seersucker shirts, special ballpoint pens, and a new miraculous medal."*
>
> **(Phone Message)** *June 21, Father's Day: "Mike took me to an early dinner at a buffet. He had thirds. Love those steroids. Then, he took me shopping in Ottawa where he bought*

himself a fishing reel and loafers. Before we got home, it was time to eat again. He wanted steak or spaghetti, likely both."

Mike wakes me countless times each night—to teach me things. Monster seems never to sleep. Everything is unpredictable, yet always the same. Night after night, the same crazed monster eyes peer into mine mandating immediate obedience. I shake. Why won't Monster sleep? I hate nights. But, somewhere behind those terrifying troll-like glares, a glimmer of Mike might surface. Though darkness hides my husband, I hold hope to the dream of seeing him one more time.

While the steroids keep him active, the sleeping pills do nothing for his agitated nights. I close my eyes and Mike hovers over me, blank-faced like those on a chiseled statue. His eyes belong to Monster. This is a replica of the nightmares I had months ago slithering through eggs and waking to a house littered in ugly.

"Get up. Get up! You need to get up," Mike demands. The urgent matters of the roof, the furnace, the investments, the checkbook, the carpet, the kids, his beer stein collection, his missing guns, his car. All addressed in the depths of the night. His, his, his–

Orders skid from his mouth, "You need to learn how to change the furnace filters." In the middle of the night, we march to the basement where he shows me how to change a furnace filter—for the third or fourth time in a single night. The next night, it might be the garage door that needs locking or the air conditioner needing a winter cover. He needs to show me. He seems to sense time is running out. Always something—like a machine that never turns off. Like a child's toy being run by someone who can't control the remote or read directions.

(Phone Message) *June 24: "Mike is busy as usual, but tires faster than he did even a week ago. He complains of a film over his eyes and asks me to read to him. Yet, this morning, he read the stock market figures from the Tribune aloud."*

(Phone Message) *June 25: "I don't see how Mike will make it through the radiation, but determination prevails. Many of you ask how you can help. If you can take him for one or more of his appointments—even just one—it would be wonderful. He needs his friends and a break from Mary Ellen's driving. Thank you all for your continued help and concern. We love all of you. Please leave your message after the beep and I will return your call."*

(Phone Message) *June 26: "Mike completed his first week of radiation. It has been very hard on him. The steroids seem to help, as each day he does something for me. Monday, he mowed the lawn with the walk-behind* *mower. Tuesday, he replaced slats in the large planters in front of the house. On Wednesday, he finished the project. He does impeccable work, but again, has difficulty making complete sentences and expressing thoughts."*

(Phone Message) *July 1: "It's the second week of radiation. We schedule six-weeks of treatment. In some ways, he seems better than a month ago. The steroids meant to shrink the growth pep him up. The anti-anxiety and sleeping pills are supposed to slow him down at night. He also takes meds for internal swelling and seizures, plus more meds to calm his upset stomach (caused by all the pills). Mike is adamant and says the pills will kill him. He hates the pills. Sometimes, catatonic, he expounds in full sentences, 'When you can't see … it's like there is a veil over your eyes … can't make the right words come out of your mouth … can't understand what's said to you … what's the use?'*

"Right after that 'downer, he says, 'Let's go to a garage sale, an auction, or Walmart.' Walmart is his request tonight, but I am taking him to a union meeting instead. That will make him happy. He will be with friends.

He still plays euchre and doesn't miss a trick. Amazing! Personality wise, he is more mellow than he's been in months. Thank the heavens!

Mike believes everyone should fish. He takes Michael's 18-month-old son David to the boat dock. Michael tags along toting the gear ensuring the fishermen will be safe. Mike shows David how to make a shish-ka-bob out of the worm. David squirms and refuses to take part in the slimy procedure. Mike continues to insist the toddler bait the hook. David holds his own, "NO." Popee relents and baits the hook for the grandson. The lessons continue all morning and into the afternoon. Relentless. Everyone must learn to fish.

Mike fishing with grandkids. Sitting: Jaclyn, Mike, Hailey and Rachel; standing: David

Popee hooks a fish and pretends to let David think he has caught one. (Years later, David, a toddler at the time, insists he remembers the day.)

"Popee put the fish in a large white bucket between us and I enjoyed playing with the fish in the bucket rather than fishing. That did not make Popee happy. Popee caught an ugly, big—at least to my toddler's eyes—black catfish and he made me hold it for a picture. I wasn't happy about that, either, but I loved the fireworks later that night," David said.

> **(Phone Message)** *July 10: "Mike begins his third week of radiation. He resents feeling sleepy all the time. Between steroids that blast his energy and the drugs to calm anger and frustration, he feels like an out-of-control roller coaster. How frustrated and depressed he must be to not comprehend and communicate. He can't remember what happened yesterday.*

"I'm on that roller coaster, too. I used to like roller coasters, but this one's not fun at all."

> **(Phone Message)** *July 11: "Mike is quiet. Says a few words, but now thanks me regularly for everything I do for him. He uses a walker. His stride wobbles. Today we went for breakfast with his family and the Olsons after radiation. He ate slower than usual. Swallowing is difficult, and he doesn't see everything on his plate. Despite his shuffle, he still wants to walk around Walmart."*

It's Walmart – again. "I want to go to Walmart to buy corn and I want to go alone. I can still drive, you know."

"Of course you can, but Dr. Brauweiler told you about state law. It prohibits driving because of the tumor. What if you have a seizure and cause an accident? You might hurt or kill someone—something you'd regret. You don't want that on your conscience."

Mike agreed. I drove him to Walmart and dropped him at the door with a reminder, "Corn only." Twenty minutes later, he came out with corn and a watermelon.

"Mike, we already have a whole watermelon in the fridge."

"Yes," he said, "that's why I bought another one. Now you'll have to eat the one in the fridge."

His logic drives me bonkers but I relish his long sentence. When we got home, exhaustion surfaced and he opted for a nap. "I'll come back to the car later and bring the groceries in," he said.

When he got up, he discovered Michael had brought the groceries in while he slept. Mike was upset. "He took my job! Why wouldn't he let me do it?"

I explained the heat of the day would have spoiled the food. Mike blasted Michael and me. "He took my job! Why is he here? I want him gone!"

Sometimes, I feel like Dustin Hoffman's mother and we are reenacting the movie, Rainman. I long for Mike, feel desperate. I miss my husband and would give anything to have him back for just one more day. His eyes are so distant.

Later, Mike asks if I would like to trade places with him.

"No, I would not. Would you like me to?"

"No," he says without hesitation, "No one should live like this." He asks, "What lies ahead?" He checks my expression, then adds, "Don't tell me."

On another Walmart adventure, we encountered a child with Down Syndrome. He later asks, "Do I look like that kid in Walmart? Do I look like that yet? When I do, please put me in a home somewhere. You will. Won't you?"

"No Mike, I plan to keep you at my side as long as I can. We'll pray I stay strong and you don't get mean."

He turned my way with a tenderness I longed for and smiled. "I could never be mean to you."

We exist. Exist. Mike allows me to dispense his meds. Meds to pep him up. Meds to keep the swelling and blood pressure down and pills to give him rest. Pills. Pills. Pills. I think about taking one of Mike's sleeping pills to experience one night of undisturbed sleep, but realize I dare not with his mood swings and my concern for others in the house.

One evening he says, "This is no way to live. I'm not taking them anymore."

He waited for me to object. I did not.

"Well?" he said.

"Well, what? You don't have to take anything you don't want to."

Mike appeared to rethink the issue. "Will I die sooner?"

"Could be. I have no idea."

"Give me the pills."

> **(Phone Message)** *July 13: "Mike spends most of his time on the deck absorbing nature. The water seems to calm him. In June, he asked about family and friends and how soon you would visit. Now, he almost never asks."*

Mike, a popular man at NICOR and everywhere else, receives tons of calls and cards. I still allow him to speak to as many friends as I can. He forgets them almost as soon as he hangs up and asks when they will call saying he hasn't heard from anyone in a long time.

Mike with his support team Steve Platko and Don Slaby

Today, the topic is rings. Rings for our daughters and our daughter-in-law. We 're back at Walmart. I cringe when I see his selections, styles he would not have selected were he whole. However, the choice of stones meets my approval—diamonds, garnets, sapphires, and zircons. Each ring under $300 and within our budget. In a normal state, he would have considered them "chintzy." Had I not reminded him long before his illness he purchased rings for all three granddaughters, he would have bought rings for them, too. He liked quality jewelry on himself and on others and he loved to see them wear it.

Mike took great pride in his clothes and expected the same from me. He preferred high-quality ironed cotton shirts and sharply creased Docker pants for the office. He had at least 40 shirts, plain colors or matched plaids. If the number got down to 30, he'd ask when I intended to iron. He wasn't above ironing himself either and if I failed to sew on a missing button, Army skills came into play and he sewed his own. With Mom there, those issues rarely occurred.

Colorblind, he'd ask if a shirt matched his pants before leaving for work. When I was angry with him for whatever reason and things didn't match, I'd nod and let him out of the house less than coordinated. I told you I was mean.

Mike prided himself on his suits for evenings out. During our five years of dating, we danced—O'Henry/Willowbrook, Aragon, Trianon, any ballroom featuring a live orchestra. Magnificent on the dance floor, I melted in his arms. We danced every dance and danced every weekend.

Flashing like the subtle silver streak in his hair, his silver-grey suit spoke class. Yummy in pink, he did not hesitate to wear it with colorful silk ties stitched by Mom. His masculinity—never in question. Dashing, simply dashing! His face, like those silk ties, was smooth and flawless. I envied his complexion, minus his Rosacea.

One Sunday each month, he'd haul out six pairs of dress shoes and shine them like bowling balls - buffed Army style while he watched football, basketball, or fishing on television. This happened monthly for 35 years. He made beds pennies bounced off of. Thoroughly Army trained.

Whether sport or dress, Mike was meticulous. Trench coat in the spring and fall, full-length black wools in winter, cashmere neck scarf, leather gloves, and a dapper hat. He always wore his silver wedding ring and when we dined out or danced, donned his dad's ruby ring.

Mom's tailoring talents, he thoroughly appreciated—suits, coats, and tux. He liked me in three-inch heels with long hair wearing a sheath dress, but didn't complain when I cut my hair or resorted to flats and jeans.

The neighborhood saw him differently. With a red bandanna tied around his forehead Indian style stressing his Rosacea covered face, he slaved like a bull and sweat like a lemonade glass in July. The white T-shirt, tight to his body, bore numerous holes. I dared not throw any of them away. His jeans bagged with a prominent plumber's crack on display.

When the yard was meticulous, he came in and cleaned house. When I'd leave a mess in the basement floral shop or stashes of paper on tables in the dining area, he'd give me three days warning, "If you can't get around to those things, I'll make time on Saturday to clean up for you."

This meant he intended to shove everything into drawers or closets knowing this would spur me to clean up before his deadline. He never did this with his things ... but then, he never made messes.

When Mom or I had guests that did not include him, he'd greet everyone sociably and disappear. Guests frequently returned to their cars to find them washed and waxed. That was Mike!

However, the downside was his jealous streak, now extremely exaggerated. Mike had one other flaw. He fed my addiction. In fact, he was the original addict. My obsession was his doing. He loved auctions and couldn't pass up cut crystal or china. Buy, buy, buy. He appreciated elegant table settings and seasonal decorating. He'd complain if I skimped on deco items in any room. Oh yes! Mom always said, "Mike vacuums the shit out of everything!" He vacuumed every room every day.

One thing for sure, when he said, "NO," the answer was "NO," and no one ever challenged him with success.

After winning a Ranger Bass Boat in a Minocqua Fishing Tournament, Mike's dream of owning a lake home came to fruition. Lake Holiday, Somonauk, IL.

II Yellow Roses and Friends

CHAPTER 11

Roaming the Roses
and
Lost at the Lake

Another day, rose bushes occupy his thoughts. He loves yellow roses. Everyone needs a yellow rose bush to remember him.

Janet went with us to the nursery. I told Mike, rose bushes do not do well in Michael's Arizona and Amy had no interest in flowers. She killed anything green. Janet would be the only one who might enjoy the gift. Ignoring my narration, he bought four, one for each of his children and one for me.

While at the nursery, Mike asked us not to tail him as he roamed the greenhouses on his own to "smell the roses." Safe he would be. As Janet and I wandered into the statuary building and admired planters, we gave Mike no thought.

A half hour later, enjoying his freedom, Mike was nowhere. Frantic, we returned to the nursery's entrance and scurried through all the buildings a second time. No Mike. My heart raced. How panicky Mike might be if he had fallen and couldn't get up. We couldn't scour the countless acres of shrubbery and trees alone and sought help from the staff.

Had Mike roamed into one of the mile-wide valleys of trees and shrubs? Could he be on the ground behind the massive spruces? If an employee were to approach him on a cart, would he cooperate?

How does one describe a man with a brain tumor without explaining his deficits? One doesn't. While easy to label his clothing, I also warned, Mike might not react well when approached. How would I describe his distant presence—eyes not belonging to an ordinary man? They were much like those of a fawn staring in a car's headlights.

I did my best to compromise the description, "The man is 60 but may appear older because of his bald head. However, he may wear a huge cowboy hat to protect him from the sun. He wears a light-colored shirt and khaki pants. He will seem 'far away.' He's not combative in normal situations, but if a stranger should make unexpected contact, he might react. He has a brain tumor." I was abrupt and to the point, all business.

Employees' guise spoke confusion. They seemed afraid. Locating tumorous men wasn't in their job description—watering, weeding, and mulching. They likely asked themselves, "And you brought him here! Why?"

They spread in all directions while Janet and I traced our steps and opened doors that said, "Employees Only." Sure enough, behind a closed door near tomato plants, Mike peered over my shoulder.

"Amen! We found him," I shouted. "We couldn't find you, Mike. You were lost and frightened us."

"I knew where I was. Right here. Why would you worry?"

What were we thinking? Like he said, "Mike was 'right here.'"

Mike wanted to go out every day, and we did. One day, Mike decided we needed to go "somewhere." He couldn't tell me where "somewhere" was. It was "there." Just "there." He expected me to understand.

"Okay Mike, we'll go when I finish the dishes, and the laundry, and get this paperwork under control. Be patient and I will take you 'there'."

Mike walked out on the deck. I figured he wanted to go to Walmart. But then, it could be the grocery store in Somonauk or the one in Sandwich or the hardware store in either town.

When I finished the chores, I went to the deck. No Mike. I yelled his name. No response. I yelled again, and again. Went to the garage. Down to the greenway. He was nowhere.

Time to call security and the Somonauk and Sandwich police. Give them the description … "Looks older than his years, bald-headed, could wear a large hat. Be slow and gentle in your approach." This time, I had no idea what he wore. Maybe khaki pants and a plaid shirt, possibly seersucker.

The kids drove in one direction. I, the other. Waiting for the police was not an option. Still, no Mike. I returned home to wait.

How could I continue to maintain the house, care for Mom, and keep my eye on him 24 hours a day? I couldn't imagine where he had disappeared to. Soon, he'd sleepwalk. Perish the thought!

People remind me, "God never gives a person more than they can handle."

After Mike's death, I checked the Bible and found people misinterpret God's Word.

> 1 *Corinthians 10:13—"No 'temptation' has overtaken you except such is common to man; but God is faithful who will not allow you to be 'tempted' beyond which you are able, but with the 'temptation' will also make the way to escape that you will be able to bear it."*

It is "temptations" that God will not allow without providing a means to escape so we can bear. The verse does not apply to "trials." God says nothing about not giving us more than we can handle. It is up to us to "handle" all things relying on God's faithfulness.

Life with Monster is no temptation. It is life, and its reality. There is no escape—except death.

As Mike would have difficulty walking in wooded areas, we ruled those zones out. Where else?

Mike had said he did not want to live like this and if he could find his guns ... no ... NO ... the lake? ... Would he?

I hurried to the water's edge. My breath shallow, I eyed the distant shore, gazed towards the deep, and turned in fear towards the boat lift. Behind Mike's boat, hidden by the canopy, Mike sat. Stoic. Lolled in his favorite fishing chair. His eyes, expressionless, fixed, and unblinking cast on Lake Holiday's cool water. He was distant and almost invisible.

"Mike! Mike! Why didn't you answer us?"

I was furious. I wanted to shake him. "Why didn't you answer when we called? We've been yelling for an hour. You scared us! Why didn't you answer!!!"

"Cause ... because ... I didn't want to."

Humm ...Why didn't I think of that?

Mike won a Ranger Bass boat in the 1987 Minocqua, WI fishing tournament which prompted the move to Lake Holiday.

CHAPTER 12

An End to Punishment

My psyche was raw. Discontent, obvious. While I journaled during the early days of Mike's illness, open wounds festered beyond limits. I wrote little. Each day, identical to the next … devastating. Words scribbled on paper turned to meaningless.

Unknown to anyone, Mom kept a dated log on Mike—useful months later in developing timelines. Her notes would jog my memory when on nine separate occasions, over many years, I tried to write this book.

Mike managed church with the walker. He couldn't get up for communion but made it through the service. He said it would be the last time he would go to church and have others see him this way. I offered to take him in a wheelchair. His pride surfaced, and he said, "No."

The rest of that Sunday was terrible. He'd walk a few steps without the walker and surrender to the wheelchair where he babbled meaningless words. He understood little.

It's all hopeless. Pointless. This Monster reduces my intelligent husband to a vegetable. I feel cheated and cannot imagine what he must feel. It's been ages since we danced. Only Monster dances.

The next day, we meet with his brothers, his sister, their mates, and the Olsons for breakfast. As we finished our meal, I wondered when new insights into brain cancer would surface and when Mike might misbehave in others' presence. So far, so good. When things progress, will he know them? They are wonderful and alter their schedules to meet with their baby brother. I acknowledge and appreciate their efforts. They do this every week.

A day later, Mike's right side reflexes are half of those on his left. At radiation, they give him heck over his alcohol consumption. They say it damages his liver.

Really! I roll my eyes. What about the drugs pumped into him? The radiation? Does not the Bible say to give drink to those who are perishing? If he wants a martini, I'll give him one. Who among these doctors have worn Mike's or my shoes? Mike is dying, I am perishing too! I will share his martini. Livers be damned. Make it a double!

Mike again threatens us who are his caregivers. Although his legs are weak, he often attempts to walk. His upper-body strength is inordinate. He terrorizes "that woman in there," meaning my mother. Says, "I want her out of there!" Monster dances more.

I'm downright angry he is hateful and want to pound sense into him. My Mike hides in there—somewhere. Another part of me cries. Mom gives us her all, and he once gave her his all. He insisted we care for her. He even declined rent saying, "Not one penny!" She lived with us for eleven years.

I don't need ALL from him anymore. I only want a tiny sliver of sanity and kindness for my mom. She too is dying. It shrouds in her eyes. You see it in her walk. Her talk. I hate Mike and the Monster within!

It pains me to recall they were best of friends and ganged up on me when I made a mess or ran late. I cannot wrap my mind around his not knowing Mom. How long before he no longer knows me or his grandchildren?

We dare not turn our backs. The frontal lobes where this evil tumor lurks control his deranged personality. Michael nor I sleep at the same time. I'm sure Michael never imagined skills learned at the sheriff's department would keep his own father in line and our family safe. It's something no child should face. Stepping in during confrontations becomes the norm.

"My dad understands little, but he knows he hates me, his only son. He refers to me as 'that man' and wants me gone. He fears me but has only physically threatened once. That didn't go well for him. I told him they trained me to handle violent criminals. If he threatened me again, I would subdue him, and make sure he died in a place he did not know, surrounded by people who did not care.

"Cruel, mean, and evil words, one of the hardest things I have ever had to do. I meant every word ... and he knew it.

"How can you love someone so much and knowingly be cruel? I'm his son and set up a fight he could never hope to win, a fight with consequences he could never live with.

"If all goes well, he'll live and die at home hating me, 'that man.' You are loved, Dad. Dearly loved. But this monster cut your phone lines to shreds, and no one is on the other end of the line to receive my words—even if I could say them. Brain tumors are ugly.

"No matter how bad my father's brain gets, he must know 'that man' will not tolerate any physical threats. His life, his future depends on it. I have one goal. Only one."

Mike's mood still changes to pleasant and cordial when his daughters or friends come. I treasure company. After one bitter argument with Michael, Mike says he wants his checkbook.

"What do you want it for?"

"I'm gonna pay for his ticket home." It is the first complete thought he has voiced in days.

"Without Michael, I cannot keep you here and you will be hospitalized for the rest of your life. Is that what you want?"

"Yes, I want him out of here and that woman (Mom) too!"

Increasingly frustrated as his illness progresses Mike constantly verbally abuses. Although he often collapses while walking, his strength is inordinate. He terrorizes "that woman in there," my mother. He wants her OUT! We dare not turn our backs.

Michael and I sleep in shifts.

Michael said he never imagined his lot in life would be this. Michael's presence alone keeps altercations from escalating—at least, most of the time. Anything and everything sets Mike off.

They warned Mike could become dangerous to himself and others even as his ability to control his own body waned. They spoke truth.

Michael doesn't mention his father's hostility. I do. Everyone saunters on eggs. No matter how softly we dance, they crack. They litter our house in ugly.

Mike mumbles. Curses under his breath as Mom passes by his chair. Mom seems neither to notice nor hear. It's as though several times each day she becomes an old plow horse with blinders on trodding from the warmth of her room past Mike's chair to the kitchen to work on the evening meal. Their eyes at no time meet.

Many nights, I kneel before Mike and lay my head in his lap. I cry. Waterworks are continual. Mike tousles my blonde hair and repeats over and over, "Buck up. Buck up. Buck up."

I don't want to buck up. I want my marriage and family back. Other nights I swaddle in confusion. He squirms in his chair as Mom passes and yells, "That woman doesn't belong in there. Get her out! I want her OUT!"

Obsession rules.

Mom's safety concerns me and Mike's language offends. Mom swears it doesn't bother her. Janet and Amy offer Mom a place in their homes, but they have two-story homes with upstairs bedrooms—an impossibility for Mom's failing heart. Nothing seems too great a task for my girls. Janet lives 50 miles away in Gardner, IL, and has two children, Rachel five and Jaclyn three. She is seven months pregnant with grandson John whom they will call Jay. Amy has nine-month-old Hailey in her arms.

My friend Colleen also offered Mom shelter in her mobile home.

My sister Lois wanted Mom in California. "I'll fly home and bring you back with me," Lois said to Mom.

Mom fussed. "I'm not going anywhere. I'm staying here." Determined and a tad stubborn.

While the steroids keep Mike active, the sleeping pills do zilch for troubled nights. I close my eyes and he hovers over me, blank-faced with eyes belonging to the fiend, the monster within his crowded skull. The only color on his face is the color of his eyes. Monster dances still more.

"Get up. Get up! You need to get up," he shouts. Urgent matters are still the same, the roof, his furnace, his investments, his checkbook, his carpet, his kids, his steins, his guns, his car, his, his, his.

I look forward to a time when he can no longer walk.

It's almost the end of July, unbelievably hot and week five of radiation. Last night Mike laid awake the entire night. He yelled and complained his legs hurt. He begged to go to the hospital, but I put him off hoping extra medication would stop the pain. We had an early doctor's appointment, and I decided we could make it till morning. Ignoring him wasn't easy. Somehow, we made it to seven and left early for radiation.

He asked to see the doctor. I agreed.

"This radiation is senseless, not helping him at all. I want it stopped," I said.

"Request denied. It's helping him. It keeps the tumor from growing!" Those words fell sharply from the mouth of a doctor who demanded control.

"Prove it! Scan and prove it!"

"No, another week of treatment. Then we'll scan."

"NO! Not another treatment until you scan."

> **(Phone Message)** *July 26: "I wish I had good news but I don't. The scan shows the tumor has tripled in size. This is OVER.*
>
> *"Before the scan, Mike called me to his side and said he could tell something major happened in his head. He motioned to the right side of his body and said he could no longer move anything on that side. His ability to grasp what is happening before doctors have a clue becomes routine. He always uses the wheelchair when he goes beyond the living room.*
>
> *"We left the hospital without radiation and celebrated. Celebrated an end to the punishment of drilling holes in his head and filling him with radiation and chemicals. Somehow, we will enjoy what little is left of life. We go to Burger King and eat crap … french fries, onion rings, lots of carbs and drink real coke. We have ice cream, too. Then, we shop at Walmart! We buy everything he wants."*

He still buys for everyone except Michael and Mom. Resilient, they remain. I do not. I cry. They don't. I no longer hide tears behind closed doors. I'm not sure how Mike feels about this trip to Walmart. It's his first trip there in a wheelchair. I wonder if he will forfeit Walmart as he has church if he has to do it from a vehicle I push.

I no longer have the courage or strength to update phone messages regularly. I'm empty. Mike is not. After each distressing marker, he rallies.

Mike's oncologist calls and suggests chemo. "He's so young. He deserves every opportunity to live. Won't you please try?"

The chemo treatments will run into thousands of dollars and likely will make him sick. Yet, I weaken and submit. Two treatments later, I stop. They do make him sick. He continues to deteriorate. I rationalize, oncologists have to make a living, too, but not at Mike's expense.

I am done and no doctor will control decisions ever again. I will not punish Mike with chemicals that make him nauseous and cause diarrhea. If these treatments provided any quality of life, I'd continue. They don't. He would not want this. No one would when they know death knocks. This is cruel. Let the poor man live the fragments of life left without inflicting more pain.

> **(Phone Message)** *July 29 "Happy day! Janet successfully delivers baby John via C-section. The following day, I take Mike in a wheelchair to Joliet to hold his grandson.*

"I lived to hold him," Mike says with a smile. "Jay (John) needs to fish."

(Phone Message) *August 7: "Last Sunday, another bright spot. When Jaclyn and Rachel came into the bedroom where he rested, he lit up like a torch slapped on his birthday cake."*

"Hi. How are you?" he said as they pounced into his bed and smothered him with hugs and kisses. A party—all about them and not about Mike and the tumor. Glorious! It's a happy day, folks."

As it nears Mom's August 24th birthday, Mike again forgets he cannot walk. He rises and then falls in the living room near a chair. He slides to the floor again the following day. Two days later, he asked for pain pills for the first time although we routinely gave them if he appeared to be in pain. He asked for two this day.

Pat and Gene Carpentier, the couple Mike wanted us to move near in Sierra Vista, AZ, visit. Mike immediately recognizes them and converses a bit, more than delighted to see them.

The kids insist I go to dinner and a movie at least once a week with one of them or a friend. I say it isn't necessary. They make me go anyway. They contend, time away will let me forget things for a while. It doesn't. However, I realize I am more patient with Mike after these outings. The kids seem to know best. Decision making is tiresome. I wish Mike were here to make decisions. Monster would like to make them. This I will not allow.

In the beginning, I had little professional help. Then, I had an aide twice a week to help with bed changes and baths. Somewhere during this stage of the mission, my children noticed the toll caregiving had on me and insisted I see Dr. Brauweiler. My guess—the kids spoke with Brauweiler or his nurse prior to my visit ... or maybe the doctor was intuitive.

"How long are you going to keep this up?" Brauweiler asks.

"As long as it takes."

The doctor shook his head and exited the room. He left without comment. I figured I had just lost my doctor as I had put him through countless hoops and jungle gyms. It appeared; he washed his hands of a defiant patient.

His nurse came in and said Doc called the insurance company to get additional help.

The office would notify me of the results. God bless concerned doctors and nurses. They soften our paths. Dr. Brauweiler phoned later that day. "I told your insurance company, if they didn't approve more help, you would also become ill and they would have two claims to address. You will get additional help."

An aide bathed Mike daily and nurse visits happened every Friday and Monday.

Mike mostly sleeps—as Dr. Handley, Mike's first doctor, said he would. Occasionally, Mike sits up on his own and tries to stand.

Summer passed and autumn threatens. It's the second of September. Mike won't give up; he continually tries to stand. Thankfully, Michael is here to lift his father's dead weight. Falls take their toll and depress Mike. His mind tells him he can do things his body cannot do.

I watch. He shrinks into his chair. Diminished, he fades into nothingness.

Having promised to keep the divorce attorney informed, I call. When I gave the receptionist my name, she put me through immediately.

“Are you ready to file,” he asks. “Had enough?”

“Thank you for your generosity—spending well over an hour with me a few months back. I apologize for waiting so long to get back with you. My life has been in turmoil. My husband has a brain tumor and has only months to live.” I blurted it out without taking a breath. I’m sure it sounded rehearsed. Bricks dumped on yet another’s head.

“I am so—so sorry. I don’t know what to say—”

“Please, there is no need to say anything or to be sorry. You couldn’t have known. Divorce or death—either way—it’s the death of a marriage. If I had left him, he would have died alone or perhaps killed someone in an accident. I am thankful to know it was not Mike who treated us unfairly. If my marriage has to end, it is better this way. I am grateful not to have it end in divorce with me hating him.”

Amy and Hailey come for a visit. Popee watches from his chair as Hailey plays. She’s been running since she was nine months old. Unable to speak, Mike grunts at Amy and points. A few seconds later, Amy finds Hailey’s toy under the couch. Popee is elated he could help and nods his upper torso in excitement.

He likes when I lay close to him. I feel poetic and tell him he is my moon and stars. I hold him close to hear his heartbeat. I want him back. I want him back! Want to see the whole of him in his eyes. Not some distant nothing. I cannot bear to think of life without him. He pats my leg reassuring I will be okay. I cannot do the same for him.

Steroids once gave him a huge appetite. Now, he eats and drinks almost nothing. Today, Mike gives no resistance when the nurse inserts a catheter with a warning not to let him remove it. He would tear and need surgery. This improves life for all of us.

A few days later, Mike becomes tense and angry. Again, he regains power, determined to yank out the catheter. It takes all of Michael's strength to hold his father down.

"Mom, get the handcuffs I brought with me," Michael yells. "They're on the garage workbench."

"No, not that!"

"Mom, I can only hold him for so long, then I will have to let go. Do you want him to rip and tear? Do you want that for him?" Michael yells … no longer soft-spoken.

"No," I said. "I do not want that."

Mike chained to our poster bed … I sob hysterically.

Michael stayed beside his father until sedation kicked in. When his father slept, Michael unlocked the restraints. My knees buckled. I sobbed more. In a lifetime, I never imagined this would come to pass.

Witnessing how easily Mike became annoyed and seeing his inconceivable strength, not once did we leave him alone.

One pair of eyes always remained on him. While Michael slept in a locked room across the hall, I laid awake beside my husband or sat on the living room couch and watched the bedroom door lest he hurt himself or someone else. I slept only when Michael sat with his father.

With steroids lowered and morphine increased, Mike does not appear to have pain.

Vicodin handles any discomfort when we see him wince, squirm, or moan. While he never voices pain, who knows?

Today again, he said he wanted to stand. I stood in front of him as he rose. He fell through my arms and caught himself on the bed. We both cried. There is no end to my tears. Henceforth, we lift Mike with a Hoyer Lift.

> **(Phone Message)** *September 5: "Rachel and Jaclyn, infatuated with the hospital bed's remote, push buttons. Head up/feet down. Feet up/head down. Popee enjoys the position change. A faint smile crosses his face. They help make his bed, prepare his food, mainly applesauce and ice cream. Sometimes, Mike lets the girls feed him. Such wonderful nurses. The girls have asked to ride on the Hoyer Lift, the swinging chair that moves Popee from the bedroom to the living room and back again, but I decided one incapacitated person per family is enough. Later, I realize I shouldhave let them.*

> *"They have watched their Popee fail by the day and it seems they understand he will not make it, but they have lost no one. How will they handle it? I lament Michael's David, a year and a half and Amy's Hailey, almost a year old, likely will not remember their Popee. How he loves them! At other times, I am thankful there will be zero possibility they will recall this nightmare."*

Monday rolls around. The nurse is here. I notice the date—September 14. Tomorrow is Hailey's first birthday. I tell the nurse Mike is dying. She says, "No, it's days—weeks—away. He's young and his body is still strong. Astrocytomas are slow growing."

She has seen many deaths. I have not. I only feel what I feel. I cannot dismiss my thoughts and share them with the children. They too are numb to "feelings."

It has been tiresome for all. I have not had a moment lately to share anything with Mom. She says nothing and continues to cook evening meals. Amazing woman. I envy her strength, intelligence, and faith. She often says, "There are many things far worse than death. Things like NOT dying."

This is one of those things worse than death Mom has experienced. This journey tarries. I pray the nurse is wrong and God will take him. At last, I do not have to be at his side as in the last day or two, he moves little and refuses water and applesauce. He does not appear to suffer. Praise God.

September 15, 7 a.m.: It's granddaughter Hailey's first birthday. Mike snores. The snoring becomes raucous. I have heard nothing like it. Is this what they call the death rattle? I call the nurse. She says it's impossible. She saw him yesterday and death is not going to happen.

"Then, what is this?" I ask holding the phone near Mike.

She comes at once and confirms death is imminent. She says parents, spouses, and those close to the terminally ill often have a sixth sense about their loved one's impending death. They discern more than the nurses and doctors.

The adult children are here. I lay beside Mike and hold him. I encourage him to go to the Father. "I release you to Him. Follow the light."

I have no tears. I beg God to take him home. The children take turns speaking final words to their father and give him permission to die as that is what Hospice advises. Hospice literature says the dying are often reluctant to "move on" fearing loved ones still need them.

> *I promised not to hold Mike to this earth! Amy admitted she told her father he should go but later said she didn't mean it. "If I could do it over, I'd just lay close and hold him."*

I rest beside Mike long after his body turns cold, leave the room, and joyfully with an awakened heart, praise God.

Mike is home. Tears come later and never end. They even spill on this book as I write—twenty years later. Mike was not a monster. He was a brave man who lived for and loved all. There was nothing he would not do for his fellow man. He breathed to serve others. He will forever breathe in me.

Michael James Aschenbrenner
Beloved Husband, Father, Popee, Son-In-Law,
Father-In-Law, and Friend
Date of Death: September 15, 1998

... *Meanwhile, Monster sleeps* ...

II Yellow Roses and Friends

CHAPTER 13

The Memorial

Mike's memorial materialized a week later in Joliet. Several hundred people attended and expressed their love and loss.

Bouquets of yellow roses and photos of Mike with family and friends lined the walls of the Carlson Funeral Home. A memorial Mass and dinner followed the next day.

Many said it was the first memorial and funeral they had attended where there was no body or casket. At Mike's request, his remains were donated to the Anatomical Society for research.

Ashes returned six months later, were buried November 5, 1999, our 38th wedding anniversary, at Abraham Lincoln Memorial Cemetery, Elwood, IL. Our children and Mike's siblings shared in the brief ceremony.

III The Second Crusade

CHAPTER 14

Mom Marian

Forty-eight hours after Mike's service, Mom asks for an appointment to speak with me. Appointment? I laugh.

"Not funny," she says, "You don't sit still long enough to talk about anything serious. I need to talk to you."

Not that I didn't sit still long enough to talk. I didn't sit still period. I wanted to be exhausted but wasn't. I went on and on like the Energizer bunny. If I could tire, I might sleep even if I didn't feel like I needed sleep. This was new. When Mike was here, I longed for sleep. Now I never slept.

Additionally, I had a crushing pain over my heart. It lasted for nearly two years. Broken Heart Syndrome or Cardiomyopathy—caused by stress, can lead to a heart attack. The condition is generally short-lived, a few weeks to a month.

Thinking it normal for my heart to bear physical discomfort following what our family had endured, I told no one.

Serious meeting indeed. We sit at the kitchen table. Mom has my undivided attention. I don't have a clue what the subject will be. Michael stands 20-feet away in the living room.

"I hate to do this to you," she begins. "It will be hard on you. I can't hang on much longer. I'm going to leave you, too."

Michael lurched across two rooms and juddered his finger at his grandmother.

"Oh no, you don't! You're not going anywhere! If you die, we'll stuff you and prop you in the corner. My mother needs you."

I love my son. We are terrifyingly alike.

Neither Mom nor Michael cracked a smile. I was too flabbergasted to comment. Mom, too, was stunned. Mom says nothing she doesn't mean. Careful with her words—she intends to die.

To Michael, she says, "Well, okay—I'll try. She turns and asks, "How long do I have to stay here?"

As though calculating the time needed to depart this earth, she asks, "How long do I have to give you?"

For God's sake, mine, and everyone else's, I want her to stay forever! "You've got to give me a year. I need at least a year," I say, not realizing how fast a year will pass.

"Okay," she says.

She rose, nabbed her walker and oxygen, and trotted to her room saying, "I'll try. I'll try."

Michael stayed on for six weeks after Mike's death. His presence and his sisters' presence were celestial. My house, full of family and friends, left me ill-prepared for the loneliness to follow.

A week after Michael and his family left for Phoenix, Janet said John had a job offer in Mishicot, Wisconsin, south of Green Bay.

Early in married life, I held Mike back from accepting promotions in other cities. I felt I had to be near Mom and my invalid father. Years later, I realized I should have honored my husband's wishes and helped my parents, too. Therefore, I encouraged Janet to follow her husband and leave Illinois.

Behind closed doors, I wept. I still weep behind closed doors. I miss my children and grandchildren. My family filled my house to the brim. Twelve in the count, Mom, Michael, Alice, David, Janet, John, and their cherubs Rachel, Jaclyn, and Jay, plus Amy, Mark, and Hailey. All were fixtures during those dark months. My household runneth over. Then, eight of them left and scattered across the country. All exited within weeks of each other.

How could Mom and Amy's small bunch fill this void? What would I do with my hours?

I learned and learned quickly. First off, I bought a riding mower and a garbage disposal. Things Mike refused to own. Then, I adopted Amy's cat Sydney. He was gentle but not a people cat. Aloof, but kept Mom company while I worked in the yard and he crawled into my lap when I sat in Mike's chair. He disliked visitors and loud voices. Still, he warmed Mom's feet and my heart.

My sleep habits lost rationale. Mike, a workaholic, had kept an impeccable house and yard. I now assumed his role. Fifteen and twenty hours of up-time were my norm. I turned into my deceased spouse. Yard, hillside, waterfront, basement, attic, jacuzzi, garage. Keep everything up–just as Mike did. Wash windows–rain or shine. Walls wiped down and polished even though they were thick, varnished cedar and a mere dust cloth on the end of a broom would have sufficed.

Mom would shake her head. If she complained, it wasn't to me. Although, she said a time or two, "You're crazy washing varnished walls." When I vaulted off a ladder in pursuit of a spotless ceiling and injured my knee, she laughed and brought me her walker. "Now, use it!" she said. She found it funny as I had "hounded" her to use her walker instead of hanging onto walls.

I raked the yard. No, make that yards—mine, the neighbor's, and the park greenway—just as Mike had done. Leaves belonging to others dare not blow into my territory. Two burn piles always blazed, mine and the one on the neighbor's drive. I'd burn at night, sometimes until three a.m. The fire contrasted the autumn's shadowy, night sky. Late-night burns became my escape tunnel.

Lake Holiday had a rule that a person must stay with all burns. No problem. I'd mosey between the two burn piles on the adjoining lots and add leaves and sticks as needed. Meanwhile, the lake's security officer sat in his vehicle on the parkway beside the house and watched the demented lady tend the fire and burn throughout the night. What was he thinking? What was she thinking?

The peaceful, fiery infernos opened heaven's skies where Mike resided. I kept the pace through the long winter after Mike's death and throughout the following year. Sydney rested on my lap when I came inside. He contented himself on Mom's bed or by sitting on our laps so long as no one hammered nails or shouted. Loud noises terrorized and sent him flying under beds.

Mom gave me more than the year she promised. She lived fifteen months after Mike's passing. The woman planned her departure.

"I can't die on Christmas. That would be too sad for you," she said. In her last few days, she repeatedly asked, "Is it Christmas yet?"

My sister Lois planned a flight in from San Francisco for Christmas Day. Mom said, "I need to be here when Lois comes. I need to ask something of her. I can't die on Christmas."

A perfectionist, Mom likely conferred with the Almighty and scheduled her demise ... the day after Christmas. I miss her as much as I miss Mike.

Marian Wagner Shoemaker

Revered and Respected ... Mother, Grandmother,
Great Grandmother,
Mother-In-Law and Dear Friend of Many

Date of Death: December 26, 1999

IV Monster's Back

CHAPTER 15

Post-Traumatic Stress Disorder

The second anniversary of Mike's death approached and passed. I grieved the losses of Mike and my mother. I faced the long, lonely winter's treacherous nights bitter, cold, and alone.

It wasn't the snow and blizzards that iced my abode. It was the Monster within.

"I'm up. I'm up. Yes, I washed the walls. The car is clean. I filled the tank, there's air in the tires, I shoveled snow, vacuumed ..."

I speak the words although my mouth does not voice them. The Monster shakes me. Macabre eyes shoot into my soul. He's real. My dead husband? No! The Monster within my dead husband! Monster screams at me!

I feel him; see him; hear him. Dare I lay a hand on him? Hide, run, do something!

I can't. Monster rules. My eyes widen. The hair on the back of my neck stands. My heart pounds. I'm dripping in sweat.

"Doesn't matter," Monster says. "You don't do anything right. Where's the checkbook? What do you mean, you don't remember? God damn it! There's only one place to put it. Top drawer. My dresser. Everything important goes there."

Monster drools. His eyes slice the room. His face angers with blackened flame. His tongue forks. It lashes, "Did you change the furnace filter? What do you mean, the stock market crashed? Are you stupid? Where's the money I left you? What do you mean, you don't remember?" His voice becomes a gruesome growl, "You were in the garage … REMEMBER? REEE-MEMBER! Our children look so different … Who are their fathers?"

Same words, same screams throughout the night. Linguistics match those that flowed from Mike's mouth. He is here. He is baaaack! I hear him; he shakes me. I feel him. I don't care if you don't believe me! My body quakes. I see him. I can touch him … almost.

God! I can reach out and put my hands on him, but please, God! Don't make me. Please, God. Make him die! It's not Mike. It's Monster. It's Mike with the Monster within!

"I'm baaaack. I'm here. Just like the doctor said. I'm going to give you another year. I'll see Christmas." The voice trails and repeats, "I'm baaaack … another year … maybe two."

Another year of shouts and sleepless nights, deadly eyes, and tremors. I cannot bear another day let alone another year of this. He is back. Monster is within. Why can't he die? If only he'd sleep.

CHAPTER 16

Monster is Alive

My body is soaked. Sopped in perspiration and terror. The bed that once provided comfort, drips in the wetness of Monster's invisible blood.

Monster is alive. His cynical voice, tangible. Sardonically suspicious, Monster slips through veiled cracks I blocked. He takes residence. Monster is within—within me. I need no doctor to tell me what has happened.

At first, he surfaces every week or two. Always the same and always different. His profile is unflawed. A perfect beast.

Each visit lasts longer than the previous one—as though Monster intends to make me his permanent home. Surely not. Isn't it fear that produces more fear? Am I the preparer of nourishing meals for Monster? Do I allow him to surface with increasing strength and demands? Am I a fertile field—a flourishing frenzy for dreams—nightmares that may never end? Will Monster consume me as he did Mike? Where's the strong woman who can handle what comes my way? Where is MY God?

Monster schedules Wednesday encounters. I remain awake in Mike's chair until my eyes can no longer stay open and plummet into bed hoping against odds Monster will not surface. Does he ever sleep?

I have not the slightest clue why Wednesday is the chosen night. A psychiatrist might discover its origin. It matters not. One night is as horrendous as any other when Monster haunts.

No one knows of these horrors. I tell no one. They need not suffer with me, but I realize I need help and attend a DeKalb County Hospice support group. We meet and share our losses and sorrows. I want these meetings to help.

They don't.

CHAPTER 17

Monster—No Match for God

Monster not dead? How is it Monster lives in my husband's body? This is not possible and yet, it is. Our war veterans have no corner on Post Traumatic Stress Disorder. It lives. It lives within me. Monster continues his routine. "I'm baaack. I'll be here at least a year."

A month into the therapy, the group leader pulls me aside. "You've had a double whammy–Mike and your Mom. No, make it multiple whammies with many family members being removed from your life." Then she asks, "Have you done any writing?"

"Yes," I say. "I am a published writer. Why do you ask?"

"I want you to try something for me. If it doesn't work, you need to seek professional, one-on-one counseling."

Her assignment—pick up paper and pen and write to this brain tumor. "I want you to give it a name and I want you to command it to die - verbally and on the paper."

"I have named it. I call it Monster and Monster is within me."

She continues. "Shout at it. Yell at the top of your lungs. Command it to die once and for all. Give it no choice. Insist it not consume you! Order it to leave your heart, body, and soul! Order it DEAD! Scream your words as you write them. Take charge. Believe them. Deal with this head on."

Humm. Where have I heard those words, "Deal with adversities head on?" From my dear mother, of course. She'd tell me, "Get your head out of the sand and deal with it."

A few days pass. I write in a journal telling Mike how I wish I could have honored his request for the end of his life to be quiet and calm—shared by only the two of us—away from everyone including family and friends. However, because of the gravity of his illness, it could not be. How saddened I continue to be for not giving him his heart's deepest wish—just the two of us.

Without warning, I rage. Screaming and writing and writing as I scream.

"You are a monster! You took Mike's life! You had no right to squeeze his brain—crush life from him. You are Satan, a MONSTER! You squeeze me as you wrenched Mike's innocent brain; destroyed him inch by inch. You are evil and deserve to die! A life for a life. Death for death. I show you no mercy. You have taken one life and you will NOT take mine. You WILL die! DIE! In the name of God. DIE! Lord, let there be light."

My screams thunder, resound off vaulted ceilings. They roar. It's a wonder I have a voice. It's cold. The doors are closed and locked. If neighbors heard, they'd alert authorities a murder was in process ... It was ... Monster's.

I heave words, "You have taken one life. You WILL NOT take mine. Die. In God's name DIE!"

Spewed lyrics boom and Sydney, Amy's cat, appears from nowhere and leaps into my arms. "Die! In the name of God DIE!" I scream again.

Syd placed his paws on my trodden shoulders and looked into my eyes. Although terrified of thunder, screams, and loud noise, Syd seized the moment. He gently and slowly kissed my flooded face one tear, one lick, one touch at a time.

Syd faced me square on for countless, endless minutes and dried every tear. I sat. Astonished.

In an instant, the instant, Syd placed his paws on my shoulders and licked my face, my sobs silenced, and tears no longer flowed. Sydney's roughened, empowered tongue removed Monster from my soul. Every tear erased; my face, completely dry. Fears bled through pores and vanished. Spirit-filled.

Syd unyielding in his charge gave one final kiss to my chin and curled beside me. We both filled with inexplicable, wondrous peace. God's peace.

How can this be? What miracle occurred? Can a loving pet be the instrument of God?

No longer am I a rose trampled on the ground. I am forever in awe. Monster, no longer within, never surfaced again. Forever dead. Peace resides. The Light has come—the Light has won.

The Monster Within

Date of Death: November 10, 2000

It has been more than 21 years since Mike's death and almost 20 years since Monster's demise. Monster no longer dances. He is not within. He is forever dead. Peace is within.

V Questions Answered

CHAPTER 18

Diagnosis Confirmed

The clues indicating Mike had a brain tumor were there. We failed to address them. Twenty years after Mike's passing, I finished writing this book, and a note fell from an old book I planned to donate. It clarified everything including the negation of the original diagnosis of Glioblastoma.

The note, written by Mike indicated Mike had seen or planned to see the nurse at NICOR before his February 1997 retirement. He did not mention it at home nor did he share its contents with anyone including Dr. Brauweiler who had found the artery (heart) blockage.

On the back of a 6-inch NICOR nurse's "Reaction Report," Mike revealed secrets confirming something was wrong long before the tumor was diagnosed. It also affirms the biopsy of a slow-growing tumor, Anaplastic Astrocytoma, was correct and negates the original diagnosis of Glioblastoma.

Twenty years! Twenty years after Mike's death ... at the exact hour I finished this book, this note surfaced! No wonder, obstacles continued to surface preventing publication. All things happen in God's time, in God's way—not mine.

Why the confusion with the diagnosis?

The original diagnosis, Glioblastoma, is a Grade 4 astrocytoma, a virulent, fast-growing brain cancer that showed Mike would pass in a few months (which he did). The size, the massiveness of this tumor, made the diagnosis appear correct and so did the three-month duration between diagnosis and death.

However, Mike's note negates all and validates the biopsy. It proves the tumor's presence for possibly years—before anyone, except Mike, knew something deadly lurked in his skull.

Mike told Dr. Brauweiler, "No. It's not here, (referring to his heart) It's here!" as his fists entrapped his skull, Mike knew what he was saying. And, when Mike said the medicine caused pain, he was also correct. It produced blood flow, food for cancer. The cancer swelled his brain.

Mom, a dress designer, seamstress, world traveler, and an avid reader with prolific knowledge of world affairs, politics, and medicine often said, "You have to know your body. Listen to it. You can tell the doctors what ails you."

After Mike's death, she handed me two articles, one on nitroglycerin, the heart medicine Mike took on his fishing trip and another on brain cancer. The first explained how nitroglycerin prevents heart attack and stroke by opening blood vessels so blood can flow to the brain. The other explained how tumors feed on blood.

Who could have known, the medicine to help his heart likely provided nourishment to the cancer in his brain?

As the tumor mushroomed and his brain swelled, there had to be excruciating pain. As Dr. Handley said, "—like an octopus squeezing his brain. It's a wonder it didn't burst."

The following note, written on a NICOR nurse's report before his February 1997 retirement (and discovered 20 years after his death), proves the tumor of long duration grew there before his retirement.

> *"Common Sense still needed periodically checked. Where am I heading. What am I feeling. The doctors will repair. Just what the heck is needed...*
>
> *A lot of women who work here in our office have asked if I knew the time I was to leave. I feel it will be another two days, even if I feel well. It is great I am not taking any medication of any kind - when I talk with nurses, I do have a problem speaking fast and*

> *accurate. I cannot go as fast as I should. My mind needs help ---I don't know why my mind is still going slow. What is delaying my thought and ideas?"*

My heart breaks knowing Mike wandered this abysmal road alone. How is it, he did not share? How is it, I can repeat his words and not have a clue what he and others who have brain disorders endure?

Steeped in the rituals of Catholicism, Mike prayed to God, the Saints, and Mary. He sought their help in attaining God's forgiveness for his wrongdoings. Yet, he refused to read the Bible, God's Word. He trusted religion to tell him what to believe instead of the Bible. After his death, I unearthed other notes from his drawers.

Another note written after his diagnosis unearthed 20 years after his death:

> *"Thank You, Lord God Almighty. Thank you for all you have done for myself and for those I pray for. I apologize for sinning and hurting You and ask You to please forgive me.*
>
> *I ask you Dear Mother Mary to please love and take care of myself and those I pray for. I thank you for your intercession and hope you will help me with the Lord. I apologize to you for all the times I've hurt you and ask you to please continue to watch over me and forgive me."*

Mike added a postscript to that litany, a prayer to the Heavens:

> *"Lord, I ask you in arbitration and kindness if you won't please continue to watch over, take care of, and protect, guide, keep well, and put your light around and on ... Mary Ellen, Mike, Alice and David, Amy, Mark, Hailey, Jan, John, Rachel, Jackie, and Baby, Mom and Dad in heaven, Mr. Shoemaker, Mrs. Marian Shoemaker. And all our family, friends, neighbors, and relatives alive and dead. ... all our property and possessions, and homes as the roof, inside, outside, and neighbors nearby, our automobiles, boats, motors, and trailers, my job, all our stand, our investment, and myself Lord."*

It was just like my Mike to put himself last, even after all his possessions. With all of them on his mind, it was no wonder he woke me countless times each night to care for his worldly goods. I humbly and most sincerely forgive him. (I will learn to forgive many times in years to come.)

Thank you Lord God Almighty

Thank you Father for all the things you have done for myself, and for those I pray for. I apologize [illegible] and hurting you, and ask you to please forgive me –

I ask you Dear Mother Mary, to please love and take care of myself and all those I pray for. I thank you for your intercession, and hope you will help me with the Lord – I apologize to you for all the things I've hurt you, and ask you to please forgive [illegible]

I thank all the Angels and Saints, to please forgive me all the things that I have done that have hurt you. I thank you for your intercession and hope you will help me with the Lord.

Lord, I ask you in [illegible] and kindness if you won't please continue to watch over, take care of, protect, guide, keep well, make well, and put your light around and on.... Mary Ellen...

MIKE, ALICE & DAVID
AMY, MARK, HAILEY
JAN, JOHN, RACHIEL, JACKIE + BABY
MOM + DAD IN HEAVEN
MR SHOEMAKER + MRS MARIAN SHOEMAKER
ALL OUR FAMILY FRIENDS, RELATIVES, NEIGHBORS, AND RELATIONS, LIVING AND DEAD.

ALL OUR PROPERTY, OUR POSITIONS AND HOMES AS ROOF, INSIDE, OUTSIDE, AND NEIGHBORS NEAR BY. OUR AUTOMOBILES, BOATS, MOTORS, AND TRAILERS. MY JOB, ALL OUR STAND, OUR INVESTMENTS, AND MY SELF, LORD

One of Mike's handwritten notes

VI Purpose in Life

CHAPTER 19

Epilogue

On a blackened, rainy night while driving toward Lake Holiday, God and I conversed.

"Why did you take Mike instead of me? He was never sick except for a ruptured appendix at 24 and a broken leg later in life. Without Mike, I don't exist. We were one. Why Lord? What, Lord? What am I to do, Lord? Show me. Use me, Lord. What is my purpose here? If you sent tribulation to get my attention, you have it!"

Wheels sloshing the wet pavement played an insistent lullaby on that wet, damp ride. The repetitive swilling sounds could have put a baby to sleep. God did not respond, so I continued to knock on His door.

"We all have a purpose. What is mine? I am alone—so alone. Use me, Lord. Give me purpose."

I attended a Bible teaching church where I learned to submit and depend on God for wisdom and guidance. I said, "God use me as You will."

> *Romans 8:28 "And we know that all things work together for good to those who love God, to those who are called according to His purpose."*

During this time, I tried on nine occasions to write this book and couldn't. Answers were missing. Words did not flow. Instead, I wrote humor stories. My life had been devoid of humor and light for a long, long time. I unearthed it and stashed Monster stories in a closet along with my sorrows.

Five years after Mike's death, reality struck. I had no one to share this life. The lake house served no purpose except to feed pride. The lake needed to go. I released it as I had released Mike and Mom.

I called Amy and said I would put the house on the market unless she and Mark wanted it. They had 24 hours to decide.

The house no longer brought joy as it did when Mike and Mom were alive. It became a prideful liability, a financial and physical noose, and it tied me to the past. I was in my 50s, too young for social security. The price of living on the lake meant a dwindling 401K. I could not maintain the property and work outside the home, too. Pride in what Mike and I had accomplished kept me there.

I loved this rural, lake community and did not want to move back to booming Shorewood or Minooka, but I realized the need to be near one of my children.

"If you and Mark do not move this way, I will move closer to you. Not something I want, but it's prudent."

Mark and Amy scrapped their plans to build in the Marseilles' woods and moved to Lake Holiday. I bought a brick home on the other side of the lake, off the water.

Soon after the move, a woman I met at church came to my door saying she was a live-in caregiver working five days a week for a home health agency. She needed a place to stay on weekends. I agreed to take her in.

One day, on our way to lunch, she dropped off time sheets at her employer's office and suggested I apply for a position with the agency.

"Never … I vowed 'NEVER.' I have done my time caring for the sick, mentally ill, and dying. I have no medical background. I'm a beautician, florist, and writer. I have no training in home health care. Never."

She reminded me I had cared for my father and mother, Mike's mom, and Mike, and bore the necessary credentials.

I walked into the agency. They hired me, provided training, did a background check, fingerprinted, and put

me to work. Perfect timing. I needed a furnace.
What prompted me to walk through the agency's doors?

Led by "someone's" hand, I floated in. Mike had said, "I want you to care for the elderly, the sick, and the dying. You're good at it." And so, I did.

I worked part time in the home-healthcare field for the next 12 years. I evolved into a caregiver of the elderly and infirm and continued to be a caregiver of words writing books and newspaper articles and leading writers' groups. Over time, I took battered women and children, a friend, a niece, and a nurse into my home. They all moved on to greater territories.

Never say, "Never."

VII Promises

CHAPTER 20

Documenting the Journey

This book needs more than purpose. It needs promise.

In 1998, the internet, a fledging of the beast it is today, offered no support during Mike's illness. I had no "go to" person or source who had lived our epic. No one to pilot us, tell us what lay ahead, no one to say what we did right or what we did wrong—no treatment options other than surgery, radiation, and chemotherapy.

Families dealing with brain tumors and brain disorders need to prepare for what they may face. When Mike's life ended, I was driven to write about our walk, but remained emotionally unprepared to document the journey—until now. It was too painful to bring to light.

In 2016, this book neared completion, and I was about to send it to editors when Amy asked me to table it and publish a book of humor first.

"Mom, people need to know the real you—if you publish Monster first, they will know you as that kind of writer.

That's not who you are. You write humor. While a book on brain disorders is important, humor it isn't."

Born to be a Star—Floating in a Galaxy of Hot Air, released in October 2016, is available through Amazon and through my website www.ahandlebarpublications.com. Born to be a Star is full of the Mike I married—fun-loving and silly, kind, giving, and considerate. The book contains versions of stories published throughout the Midwest.

Terrors and Travels and Volume II of Born to be a Star—(Still) Floating in a Galaxy of Hot Air will follow. In Terrors and Travels, I thwart an abduction on a plane over the Hawaiian Islands and hit into embezzlement in a school district. Someone threatens, "You will be murdered and raped—in that order." All books are nonfiction.

The Monster Within was further delayed after agreeing to work with Dr. Reno Caneva of Lockport, IL on his book, Dellwood Chronicles; released May 2018.

Had I published The Monster Within in 2016, integral parts of this book would have remained unknown as in 2018 Mike's notes surfaced to reveal how long the brain tumor had existed also confirming its correct diagnosis. In 2016, I was also unaware of the immune system's role in curing cancer. The publication's delay became a blessing allowing this information to be included.

CHAPTER 21

Giving Hope

Scientists work towards a cancer cure. Yet, surgery, radiation, and chemo, the same therapies that have been the powers at hand for countless years, continue. While they prolong most lives, they are not considered cures. Cancer cells remain despite these treatments. They live in all of us.

These treatments are in different forms using different chemicals. All take tolls on the kidneys, liver, heart, and pancreas. They kill both cancer cells and healthy cells. They destroy immune systems.

Meanwhile, scientists agree—it takes a mighty immune system to recover from these treatments. NO ONE beats cancer or overcomes the side effects of these treatments without a powerful immune system.

Happy thoughts! Hundreds of studies and trials are underway. October 1, 2018: The Nobel Prize for Medicine (research on cancer) was awarded to James P. Allison of the US and Tasuku Honjo of Japan for establishing what is called, "a game-changing, landmark"—discoveries in the fight against cancer by harnessing/manipulating the immune system.

The Nobel committee said, "Treatments are often referred to as 'immune checkpoint therapy,' unleashing the body's own immune cells and have fundamentally changed the outcome for certain groups of patients with advanced cancer."

Allison and Honjo both worked independently on proteins that act as "brakes" on the immune system which prevents the body and its main immune cells, known as T-cells, from attacking tumor cells.

This discovery was the "brake" needed to release immune cells to attack tumors. Each doctor discovered different proteins that act as a "brake" by using different mechanisms.

Britain's University of Manchester immunologist Dan Davis described it as a game-changing cancer therapy that sparked a revolution in thinking about the many other ways in which the immune system is harnessed or unleashed to fight cancer and other illnesses.

One US research hospital's recent report on immune therapies for various cancers said there is tremendous potential shown by immune therapies—especially in cancers of the blood and Lymphoma. However, its use in Glioblastomas has not been hopeful. Glios remain stubborn cancers.

The survival rate for Glio and Astro patients is not as promising as it is for other cancers. For now, it's all about survival. Glioblastoma survivors live an average of 11 to 15 months following diagnosis. Astros live longer depending on the grade and location of the tumor. Yet, I have read testimonies from individuals living longer than 10 years using varied "cures."

However, once the brain is "invaded," whether by chemicals, radiation or by a surgeon's knife, the patients are "compromised." The degree of this "compromise" varies. Many suffer from brain dysfunction, poor or lack of speech, decreased mobility, and incontinence. Quality of life becomes questionable.

Stem cell therapy also holds great promise.

A bright light in the darkness of brain cancer is Olympic skater Scott Hamilton. His "incurable" brain tumors continue to shrink. Miraculous. Read all of his inspiring books.

Dr. Ben Williams, Ph.D. has survived a Glio for 23 years. He credits Temodar being added to his chemotherapy. Read his book, Surviving Terminal Cancer.

Thomas Jefferson University Hospital, Philadelphia, is testing an experimental immunotherapy vaccine for Glio patients. In terms of survival, there was a significant improvement in the 33 who participated in the trials.

The vaccine is made from the brain tumor right after it's surgically removed. The tumor cells are engineered to attack the left-over microscopic cancer.

One chamber reportedly holds a million cells. The vaccine goes into a diffusion chamber that's implanted in the patient's abdomen. As the contents spread in the body, the immune system gets reprogrammed to kill cancer.

Researchers say until it's proven that this immune therapy works alone, they advise patients to have standard radiation and chemotherapy—that generally do not work.

There's preliminary evidence the therapy could also work for other malignancies, including pancreatic and lung cancer.

CHAPTER 22

Nature's Miracles

To date, no magic pill or treatment guarantees a cancer cure. Even when a surgeon removes a tumor and tells the patient they have removed the entire tumor, he advises follow up chemo and/or radiation.

What he doesn't tell the patient is ... cutting into the mass aggravates cells and two percent of those cancer cells—the same as the ones he removed—continue to fester and that is why more chemo and radiation may be advised.

Without a strong immune system, additional chemo and radiation will still fail.

According to internet reports, the cancer death rate has improved only five percent since the 1950s and the average cancer patients can expect their treatment bills to be around $300 thousand.

Oncologists benefit financially from prescribing chemo. A private oncologist derives two-thirds of his/her income from prescribing chemo.

Healthy Immune Systems

It didn't take a Nobel Prize winner to discover ways to develop a hefty immune system. The internet, laden with examples of individuals who have beat cancer by using their own immune systems without pills, chemo, and radiation, fosters hope. It's up to readers to do the research. Countless options to treat different cancers! Nutrition and natural remedies play in recovery.

Other countries appear to be more advanced than the US in using natural/alternative cancer treatments. In less affluent countries, where there is less government control, successful, natural cures have come to the forefront. It could be because funds for research (Pharma) are not as lucrative as they are in the US. This forces patients to turn to natural remedies—remedies that work! Pharma does not support herbs, vitamins, and food. There is no money there for doctors or the pharmaceutical industry.

Even if one opts for the traditional treatment that kills both cancer and healthy cells, there is zero doubt, survival depends on one's ability to rebuild the immune system.

During my research, I discovered "fever-inducing" as a treatment for many cancers and other illnesses. An episode 30 years ago in my late husband's family gave validation.

I asked Mike's cousin Jane if her sister Agnes died from Lupus.

"No," she said, "Ag died from heart failure. Her Lupus 'burnt out' last winter when she had a fever over 104."

I found her statement odd and dismissed it. Now, I read it in medical books and see it on the internet.

Professor of Radiation Oncology, Dr. Baldassarre Stea and researchers at the University of Arizona, Tucson, say they have found the clue why some Glio patients live longer than others.

They say clues lay in the RNA (found in DNA) of short and long-term patients. His team looked at the genetic variation in about three dozen patients and found a gene called WIF1 is distinctly higher in patients who survive longer. Those who lack the gene succumb to the diseases much quicker. They hope to use this test as a predictor of survival time, who will need more or less treatment, and use it for therapeutic purposes to help Glio patients live longer.

The aggressive Glioblastoma killed Sen. Ted Kennedy in 2009 and Sen. John McCain in August 2018.

Despite the research and hope the medical field speaks of, the Los Angeles Times and the McGill Cancer Center in Montreal oncologists' surveys show 75% to 91% of oncologists would refuse chemotherapy as a treatment for themselves or their families because they are "too toxic and ineffective."

Why then are 75% of all cancer patients urged to take chemotherapy by their oncologists?

More Promising Research

Creighton University School of Medicine, Nebraska, revealed supplementing with vitamin D and calcium can reduce your risk of cancer by an astonishing 77 percent. This includes breast, colon, skin and other forms of cancer.

Creighton's study involved 1,179 healthy women from rural Nebraska. They gave one group of women Calcium (around 1,500 mg daily) and vitamin D (1100 IU daily) while another group received a placebo. Over four years, the group receiving the calcium and vitamin D supplements showed a 60 percent decrease in cancers.

In just the last three years, the study reveals an impressive 77 percent reduction in cancer because of supplementation. This research provides strong new evidence that vitamin D is the single most effective medicine against cancer, far outpacing the benefits of any cancer drug known to modern science.

Websites assist in decision making on ways to beat cancer. Helpful Websites include Chris Beat Cancer and The Truth About Cancer.

Chris, a 26-year-old with stage-four colon cancer, had surgery but did not follow with chemo or radiation. He used alternative medicine (food among other things) to boost his immune system, FIGHT and WIN. His methods will be helpful to anyone, regardless of the treatments chosen. Chris is a long-term survivor. Also, read Philip Day's, Cancer: Why We're Still Dying to Know the Truth. Also research SP-5.

Internet brain tumor support groups provide information and encouragement. A seven-and-a-half-year Glio survivor in the United Kingdom started Survivors to Thrivers."

Administrators of the site include a 15-year survivor, the adult child of a 2-year survivor, a nurse with a Glio, and the aunt of a survivor. Many in the group have other types of brain cancer (other than Glios and Astros) All are welcome and encouraged to join.

The group is less than a year old and has more than 60 long-term survivors. Three have survived up to 20 years and are still living. It is a positive place for information, sharing tips, support, optimism, and hope around the world.

If cancer lurks, take no one's word that surgery, chemo, and radiation are the only options. There are other treatments that will cause no harm—choices Mike and I did not know of.

Modern medicine tried and modern medicine failed us. Also lacking in our cascade of horror was an untiring, unwavering relationship with God. Our journey would have been far different and peaceful had we leaned on Him.

Climb every mountain. Rest in the valleys and "Never say 'never'."

Find your hope … Find your cure … It's out there.

Above all—find God. If you look, you will find Him.

To every thing there is a season, a time to love...a time to break down...a time to weep...a time to mourn...a time to keep silent, and a time to speak. It is time.

CPSIA information can be obtained
at www.ICGtesting.com
Printed in the USA
LVHW050621130819
627414LV00004B/11/P

9 780997 657524